your
ONE-YEAR-
OLD

Books from
The Gesell Institute of Child Development

Infant and Child in the Culture of Today
Gesell, Ilg, Ames, and Rodell

The First Five Years of Life
Gesell, Ilg, Ames, and others

The Child from Five to Ten
Gesell, Ilg, Ames, and Bullis

Youth: The Years from Ten to Sixteen
Gesell, Ilg, and Ames

Child Behavior
Ilg and Ames

Parents Ask
Ilg and Ames

School Readiness
Ilg and Ames

Is Your Child in the Wrong Grade?
Ames

Stop School Failure
Ames, Gillespie, and Streff

Child Care and Development
Ames

The Guidance Nursery School
Pitcher and Ames

Don't Push Your Preschooler
Ames and Chase

Your Two-Year-Old
Ames and Ilg

Your Three-Year-Old
Ames and Ilg

your
ONE-YEAR-
OLD

The Fun-Loving, Fussy
12- to 24-Month-Old

by Louise Bates Ames,
Frances L. Ilg, and Carol Chase Haber
Gesell Institute of Child Development

Illustrated with photographs by Betty David

A DELTA BOOK

A DELTA BOOK
Published by
Dell Publishing Co., Inc.
1 Dag Hammarskjold Plaza
New York, New York 10017

For information address Delacorte Press, New York, New York.
Delta ® TM 755118, Dell Publishing Co., Inc.

ISBN: 0-385-29206-6

Reprinted by arrangement with Delacorte Press
Printed in the United States of America

9   8   7   6   5

To the memory of
JOAN AMES CHASE

CONTENTS

your
ONE-YEAR-
OLD

chapter one

YOUR INFANT BECOMES A TODDLER

Your boy or girl is officially a One-year-old until the time of that second birthday, when he or she becomes officially a Two-year-old.

At the time of his important first birthday your infant is a treasure and a joy to all concerned. Your typical Twelve-month-old tends to be an extremely lovable little person— friendly, sociable, amenable. Given a reasonably favorable personality, normally good health, and a modestly supportive environment, most One-year-olds seem to adapt rather easily to whatever it is the adult caretaker has in mind. And it is usually easy for the adult to adapt to what the baby has in mind.

Your Two-year-old also should be fun. By the time he is Two he will have much to say. He will tend to like other people and to appreciate their attention. He will cuddle and kiss. He will, on request, proudly show you his eyes, his nose, his mouth, his arms, his foot. He is excited about what he knows and what he can do. He loves to have you play with him, and he usually does his best to please you.

He can feed himself, even though messily, and he tends to cooperate when you dress and change him. In short, most of the time he is a real pleasure to those around him.

All this being true, with One so delightful and Two so terrific, we might anticipate that in the months between your child's first and second birthday, with locomotion and a certain amount of language among his new abilities, life would become ever easier.

Is this the case? Do children move smoothly through these special months, merely getting bigger and more capable as they approach Two? Not at all.

Certainly, as a child moves from Twelve to Fifteen, Eighteen, and Twenty-one months of age his vocabulary grows, his ability to handle objects increases, and he becomes more mobile. Getting around is no longer restricted to creeping on all fours or cruising beside stable objects. Now your toddler can walk around the house, run, and get up and down the stairs with ease.

It is indeed true that many children during this second year of life seem to advance light-years in their basic abilities. *But* they do not necessarily become easier to live with. As human behavior develops, often the negative parts of a personality show themselves before the positive. You will find that most little boys and girls tend to say "no" before they say "yes," throw things before they become interested in picking them up, run away from you before they are able to respond to "Come here, dear."

In fact, much of any child's effort, in the second year of life, seems to be devoted to building up his or her own independent way of doing things, and that way is much of the time the exact opposite of what you, the parent, have in mind.

So passing the Twelve-month mark and graduating from infancy do not by any means imply that your child is about to settle down. On the contrary, he seems eager to exercise his new powers. He becomes demanding. He strains at the leash. While being dressed, he may now have to be held bodily. In his chair he stretches forward demandingly toward things he can't reach. He wants to hold and carry something in each hand, or he may *himself* want to be carried even after his increasing weight makes him something of an armful. And he is beginning to insist on doing things for himself.

We may think of life for the One-year-old as a building wave which crests around the age of Eighteen months. Even by Fifteen months this wave of increasing egocentricity, demandingness, and opposition is well on the rise. Just getting the child of this age through his or her daily routines is no picnic.

At Eighteen months of age, which we shall especially emphasize in this volume, this hypothetical wave will crest. Then, on its way toward the calm which usually comes at about Two, the child will go through the Twenty-one-month-old stage. Whether this age zone will be smooth or stormy depends largely on the individual child. If well advanced in behavior, he or she may be approaching the calm and smoothness of Two. If the child is less advanced, Twenty-one months can be as stormy and difficult as Eighteen months.

Overall, though, parents will find their One-year-old's increasing abilities in all departments a source of pleasure and pride, even though the negative side of his personality will be tough to deal with. Whatever your child's temperament, the twelve months which follow his first birthday will be full of surprises. It will be a time when you will need all the ingenuity, all the resilience you can muster. We hope the information we give you in this book may help make this often tumultuous year of living go more smoothly than it otherwise might.

chapter two

WHAT YOU SEE IN EARLY INFANCY CAN HELP YOU UNDERSTAND LATER BEHAVIOR

It is probably fortunate that babies are infants before they are anything else since infants teach us many lessons which, if well learned right at the start, will stand any parent in good stead through the long years of childhood.

Of the two main lessons which your infant will teach you, the first is that nothing you do will substantially speed up his development. Various abilities will appear when they are programmed by nature to appear. Just as you cannot speed up your child's teething, you cannot, even by serious efforts, substantially speed up the time when various behaviors will make themselves evident.

The second major lesson is that every infant and every child is an individual, different in major respects from every other. Parents can help children fully express their positive characteristics and can usually discourage them from some of their less positive traits. But as a parent you cannot determine what your child will be like.

A third important lesson which any infant can teach you is that *you* do not have to *teach* him how to perform many of the basic tasks of living. Your child will eventually sit alone with only modest encouragement from you. He will crawl and later creep without your showing him how.

Though you may in your enthusiasm encourage such baby games as pat-a-cake, the actual basic motion that underlies this game (patting the hands together in a horizontal movement of the arms) comes into the infant repertoire quite naturally and without demonstration from you.

The vitally important, and exciting, matter of individual differences will be discussed at some length in Chapter Nine. Here we would like to emphasize the important fact that in most cases, even with rather vigorous and well-intentioned efforts, parents cannot substantially speed up any of the usual infant behaviors.

Numerous research studies at the former Yale Clinic of Child Development by Dr. Arnold Gesell and his staff have established this fact conclusively. Using identical infant twins as subjects, research was carried out to find out whether or not behavior could be sped up. Kinds of behavior checked on were stair climbing, block building, language, and other basic behaviors.

At just about the time when a new behavior might be expected to appear but neither twin had as yet exhibited this behavior, one twin was trained rather rigorously in the performance. The other twin was not presented with the situation (stairs, blocks, or whatever) until the first twin had been trained for several weeks.

In a typical instance, when both twins were Forty-six weeks old and neither had as yet climbed or attempted to climb stairs, one twin (T for Trained) was given six weeks' encouragement and practice on the stairs. By the end of this period she was climbing proficiently. The other twin (C for Control) was kept in a living situation where there were no stairs for the six weeks of T's training and was then introduced to the stairs when she was Fifty-two weeks old.

Within a day she was climbing as effectively and even with the same hand-knee pattern as her twin, even though she had not earlier seen stairs and had not seen her twin climbing them.

Studies like this have convinced us that at approximately the time when a new behavior would be appearing, added age is quite as effective as diligent training in causing that behavior to make itself evident.

So, if you really cannot speed up behavior appreciably, and if you really do not need to teach your child such basic behaviors as crawling and creeping and block building, what can you do? What should you do? Certainly it is the nature of the parent to want to help his child's development, and most young parents are strongly motivated in this direction.

Our best suggestion, when it comes to infancy, is to spend a lot of time with your baby; be enthusiastic and interested. For most parents this is usually not too difficult. Play with him or her in ways which come naturally to you.

You do not need much learning equipment or fancy toys.

Babies like to be noticed. They like to have you hold them, and rock them, and talk to them, and sing to them. They like the things which a loving parent does quite naturally.

Your baby will crawl and later creep even if you don't do much about it, but your enthusiastic approval of his successes will encourage him to repeat those activities which give both you and him a great deal of pleasure.

Though you do not need to teach your baby to read or count or spell or do arithmetic problems, as some psychologists suggest, you *are* teaching him all the time by just being with him and playing with him. You are teaching him that he is a valuable and loved individual, that grown-ups are supportive and helpful, that the world is good.

It may help you most, in appreciating what to do, to realize that a baby's mind is not separate from the rest of him. He does not have to be vocalizing to tell you that his mind is at work. As he lies on his back and watches his waving hands, he is learning about the world. As he creeps toward and reaches a ball and brings it to his mouth, he is learning about the world. Very, very early he learns how to get the nourishment he needs, how to get the attention he desires.

But babies, probably even more than Eighteen-month-olds, need time to themselves. It is possible to smother a young baby with attention, particularly if the whole family sits around and constantly admires his accomplishments. He needs time to himself as well as time with you. He will tell you, very clearly, when he *does* need you.

Your time with your infant should be, so far as you can make it, a time of relaxing pleasure and enjoyment. He will learn all he needs to from the things which you as a parent do with him and for him quite naturally. You really do not need to read a book to find out how to live with, and love, your baby.

All these lessons can be of tremendous help later on. It is relatively easy when your child is still an infant to accept the fact that you cannot, and need not, speed up his development. Your baby doesn't creep yet? So be it. He lacks words to express his needs? You feel confident that words will come in time.

Most parents are not really tempted to rush the development of their infants. When the child is older and the temptation to hurry things along is greater, it's a good idea to remember the patience and acceptance you felt when your child was an infant.

The same acceptance is important when thinking about the second lesson of infancy—that one cannot substantially change a child's basic personality. It is crucial that you try to accept your child for who he is, not who you would like him to be.

And lastly, when it comes to teaching there are many things which one does need to teach a child as he grows up. But remember that basic age changes do come and go on their own. Dr. Gesell once commented, "Environmental factors modulate and inflect but they do not *determine* the progressions of development."

chapter three

GENERAL CHARACTERISTICS OF THE AGE

There is nobody in the world more lovable, more unmovable, more implacable, more challenging, more difficult to live with than your "typical" Fifteen- to Twenty-one-month-old child.[1]

Chubby body, rounded cheeks, silky baby hair, head-forward tottering stance, this lovable little child bumbles around like a baby bear. You want to hug him, but he may not want to be hugged. You want to hold him in your lap, but he may not want to be held.

You may be dying to play with him, entertain him, show him what a treasure you consider him to be. He, however, may be entirely engrossed in his own activities, like pounding away with his favorite "bang bang" (hammer). Eighteen months is an adorable age, but it can also be a difficult one, for both parent and child.

It will at times be frustrating to you that you cannot

---

[1] Since many of the admittedly fascinating egocentric and strong-minded characteristics of the period between One and Two years of age come to a head at Eighteen months, we shall in this chapter talk specifically about the Eighteen-month-old. But the behaviors we describe are on their way at Fifteen months; are receding a trifle by Twenty-one months. Thus, to a large extent, in many, the things we talk about here will apply to boys and girls all the way from Fifteen months right through Twenty-one months of age.

show him your affection and that you want to be his friend. It will almost certainly frustrate him when he realizes that he doesn't have the words or the motor skills required to carry out his urgent plans. So, when he becomes the most frustrating to you, try to remember that life is often extremely frustrating for him.

There is hardly anything in the world more exciting than something which is on the verge of becoming. When this something is a human being, a human personality on the verge of declaring itself, the excitement doubles.

Admittedly the potential is there when the sperm meets the egg. But we as parents and grandparents see, or imagine that we see, the person emerging more clearly at about Eighteen months than at any succeeding age. Later on the child will have become. Right now he or she is becoming.

When he is no longer a baby but is not yet a preschooler, his very in-betweenness on good days can be a delight to behold.

It may, or may not, help in thinking about your child of this age to know that when a chimpanzee and a child are brought up together in the same household, so far as most abilities are concerned, they turn out to be rather equal until around Eighteen months of age. Only after that does the human infant move appreciably ahead of the chimpanzee.

So it is only at some time after Eighteen months that we see what some have called the truly human thing—that is, the child who begins to behave in those particularly human ways. It may help you recognize and respect your child's immaturities, and help you not expect too much, if, even though, of course, he actually *is* a human being from the time he is born, you think of him as if he were somewhat prehuman.

If the Eighteen-month-old who enlivens and complicates your household is your very first child, the whole experience may be somewhat bewildering. The typical child of this age can be seen as enchanting if the viewer appreciates an almost total egocentricity, but it will be frustrating if one is looking for a warm emotional response and ready compliance.

What a funny little creature he is! How dear and yet how difficult. A baby you can cuddle and coo over if that be your pleasure. By the time he is Two or Three years of age you can talk to and even play with your child. Eighteen months is somewhere in between.

A child of this age may insist on having his own way, may become suddenly very grabby about possessions. He may even fight with the dog over a desired object, for instance, both pulling at opposite ends of an afghan.

And yet this fighting is somehow different from that of the typical Two-and-a-half-year-old. The latter seems really to want the specific object itself. At Eighteen months the child seems somehow to be gathering everything (in-

11

cluding even the arm of the chair he may be sitting in) into his orbit of influence. He seems sometimes to want *everything,* to prefer that everybody else have nothing. Even his staring glances give the impression that he is trying to pull everything he sees into himself.

Much of the time he bumbles around in an independently aimless way until some object or person (especially a sibling) gets in his way. Then he may become very set on this one thing and stubbornly try to have his own way at any cost.

This is perhaps the age above all others when sheer motor behavior takes over. One might almost say that the child of this age thinks with his feet. That is, he barges around, motor-minded, and often only when he bumps into an object does he stop and examine it. He does not as a rule, as he will when older, spy an object and then walk toward it.

The same may even be said of his social activities. Often he notices some other child only when he has bumped into him. Then he may poke that child, push him, pull his hair, as if by sheer motor manipulation he will find out what this other young person is like.

Later he will gauge spaces to see if they are large enough for him to maneuver before he attempts entrance or exit. Now he lunges up to some small opening and tries to project himself or his toy through an often too tiny space.

The child of this age is not only very self-determined but at the same time very vulnerable to the environment. Almost anything may attract his attention, and then he almost seems to have to respond, without rhyme or reason. But once he has made up his mind to do something or not to do something, unless your tricks and techniques plus a lot of sheer luck move him in the direction of your choice, you are pretty much out of luck in trying to switch him. Once he makes up his mind, he will hang on for dear life, unless, and this is part of his unpredictability, he forgets or loses interest in what he is doing. Behavior at this age is characterized by these two extremes: total persistence or its extreme opposite—moving rapidly from one thing to another almost without purpose.

Conclusions are very important to the child of this age. He or she likes to close a door, hand you a dish, close a book; likes to be chased and caught. He shows a strong love of opposites. In fact, he is quite as likely to do the opposite of what you ask as to obey your suggestion. He dumps the wastebasket instead of putting things into it; takes his clothes off but cannot put them back on; runs away from people who call him. He even loves to walk backward or pull his carriage backward. We often describe him as walking down a one-way street, and his direction tends to be the opposite of what the adult has in mind.

Emotionally, as in other ways, your boy or girl tends to be uneven and unpredictable, given to rather violent displays of temper. Emotional behavior the child of this age does display, but it is not well modulated. The Eighteen-month-old, if he does not like something, cannot yet merely limit himself to a frown or pout. Rather, he is all too likely to put on a full-fledged temper tantrum over what may actually be only a minor frustration. He very likely does not truly mean all those tears and tantrums. It is just that his body takes over. He may, in fact, hit or kick everything in sight. He may get so tangled up in himself that some days almost nothing goes right.

The child of this age is extremely self-involved. He relates to others if and when it pleases him. If attractive and normally cheerful, he may merely look rather sad at times. If less attractive and characteristically sober, he may actually look like an abandoned waif in his moments of withdrawnness. Even when not looking unhappy, the child of this age may look somewhat bewildered—as if he were observing more than he could take in.

If he is frustrated, his most usual response may be to yell rather than to seek a solution, though he may turn to the adult with just a soft cry or *eh-eh.* He may also, even like a grown-up, kick or hit a chair or other object if it does not work the way he wants it to.

At this year-and-a-half stage, boy or girl is on the verge of much that is new and exciting. For the moment, however, the child is only on the verge and needs much help, emotionally as well as in other ways, from those around him. He needs to be protected from his own impulsivity. It is not unusual for the child to dash out into the street. The notion that a car might run over him seems quite beyond his comprehension. Unfortunately he does have the motor ability to get out into the street if he is not constantly watched.

He quite typically says "no" instead of "yes," "down" instead of "up." All this makes him more than a little difficult to deal with, though actually even his kind of defining things by calling them the opposite of what they are marks a new maturity compared with the time around his first birthday when he was on a more positive beam.

So that all this doesn't sound too negative, we must add that there are times when the child of this age shows overwhelming affection for his parents, a doll or teddy bear, or even, occasionally, a new baby in the family. Not only can he be affectionate, but there is at times something almost flirtatious, certainly roguish, about his smile. Except when he is being his most difficult, he may seem extremely lovable to others. He seems especially attractive when "fetching" something that belongs to some member of the family or when he is imitating some simple household task.

Our observation of the development of emotional behavior in the growing infant and child has revealed that from earliest infancy on, ages of emotional equilibrium tend to alternate with ages of disequilibrium. These changes in emotional stance, though they can be improved or made worse by environmental factors, seem to result chiefly from changes which go on within the child's body.

Though children differ as to the extent to which they express these emotional changes, in general the timing is somewhat similar from child to child.

So, as Figure 1 shows, around Forty-four weeks of age

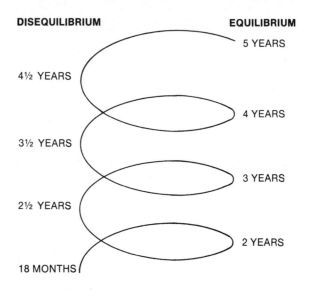

Figure 1
Alternation of Ages of Equilibrium and Disequilibrium

many infants tend to go through a brief period of disharmony, a disharmony which in most resolves itself in the
good equilibrium of the just One-year-old. Briefly around
Fifty-two weeks (or Twelve months) of age many enjoy a
period of calmness and satisfaction.

In the age zone of Fifteen months to Twenty-one months
they once again tend to be rather difficult. Wishes and
needs are strong, but the child's ability to satisfy these
wishes and needs is often far from adequate. One must
expect some stormy days at home, days which for most
children resolve themselves very nicely somewhere
around the time of the second birthday.

When the child is Two, his body seems to work for him
in a way which is more predictable, effective, and satisfactory than at Eighteen months, when he often stumbled
and fell, when hands did not always do just what he
wanted them to. The Two-year-old also has the kind of
language often lacking just earlier, language which allows him to tell you what he wants and needs. And the

Two-year-old seems calmer, happier, on a more positive emotional plane than just six months earlier. In fact, the stage of disequilibrium so characteristic of many Fifteen- to Twenty-one-month-olds happily resolves itself as do other stages of disequilibrium, given just a few additional months of growing.

chapter four
ACCOMPLISHMENTS
AND ABILITIES

This chapter will describe some of the outstanding accomplishments and abilities, especially motor and language abilities, of the typical child in that dramatic time between his or her first and second birthdays. We shall tell you a little about behavior in each of the four quarters of this year, filled with changes.

As before, we'll concentrate on the Eighteen-month-old. We have chosen to emphasize this particular age because it represents a significant halfway point between these two important birthdays and also because it is one of the most difficult ages to live with and one of the least understood ages in this very special year. We believe that parents of the Eighteen-month-old boy or girl need all the help they can gather.

ONE TO TWELVE MONTHS OF AGE

In the first four months of life most infants lie on their backs. Eyes are active, arms may wave, legs may kick, but the range of postural and prehensory abilities is limited indeed.

In the second quarter year (Sixteen to Twenty-eight weeks of life) most babies begin to sit, and this often becomes their favored posture. Baby sits, at first well propped, but by Twenty-eight weeks most can sit unsupported except by their own hands.

A tremendous advance comes in the third quarter of this first year (Twenty-eight to Forty weeks). Now the child no longer needs to prop himself with his hands, so they become free to grasp any object available. This sitting unsupported and the grasping and manipulating of objects make the child seem infinitely more mature than just a few months earlier, when he was quite content to lie supine. Not only in sitting but in lying on his stomach, the baby expresses wonderful new skills. First he pivots, and then he crawls, pulling his weight forward over his forearms, though his legs and abdomen, still drag on the floor. As he moves toward Forty weeks, he manages to get both knees under his abdomen, which he can now push up well off the floor. This prepares him for his next big move—the actual ability to creep on hands and knees.

The final quarter year (Forty to Fifty-two weeks) is marked by rapid and skillful creeping. Now no part of the house is safe from your young adventurer. Hands are increasingly active, increasingly helpful, as he manipulates now this object, now that; but creeping about from spot to spot may be his favorite activity.

TWELVE MONTHS

And now comes that glorious time of the first birthday. Now that he is a more than skilled creeper—he takes this activity very much for granted—the drive toward pulling himself upright and, if possible, taking a few steps supersedes all other activity. Some still need substantial support. They either cruise along beside the rails of their playpens or accept adults' hands. Others already can manage those first steps alone. When this is the case, their pride in accomplishment, even when walking is very unsteady and tottering, is seen clearly in their joyous smiles.

Hands now move skillfully in their manipulation of objects. Now that pincer prehension—grasping objects between thumb and forefinger—is possible, grasping even tiny objects is sure and secure. These babies like to grasp, and they love to release, dropping whatever it may be that they are holding, with full expectation that you will pick it up and return it to them so that they can release it once again.

Most will even attempt, in imitation of your own demonstration, to make a tower of two small blocks, though this major new move will be a little beyond the ability of most for another two or three months. But hands are quite skilled. The Twelve-month-old baby picks small morsels of food from his tray with deft pincer prehension. Finger-feeding comes before self-spoon-feeding, but the year-old infant may seize a spoon by the handle and brush it over his tray. He can also dip a spoon into a cup and release it.

The year-old baby loves an audience. This is one reason why he is so often the very center of a household group. He likes to repeat performances laughed at. He enjoys applause for such new abilities as waving bye-bye or his well-perfected pat-a-cake. Your applause seems to help him sense his own identity. He is defining a difficult psychological distinction—the difference between himself and others.

And he is capable of primitive kinds of affection, jealousy, sympathy, anxiety. He may be responsive to rhythm. He may even show a very slight sense of humor, for he laughs at abrupt surprise sounds and at startling incongruities.

Fifty-two weeks is clearly the heyday of sociability. The child of this age enjoys social give-and-take. He enjoys his carriage ride, enjoys standing up in his harness, and is especially interested in moving objects such as automobiles and bicycles. At home he enjoys hiding behind chairs to play the game of "Where's the baby?" Language is developing nicely. Now in addition to his earlier "Mama" and "Dada" he has several further "words" in his vocabulary. He may be inhibited by a firm "no, no." Language, both active and responsive, is still fragile, but it is clearly budding, even though not yet quite ready to blossom.

FIFTEEN MONTHS

The Fifteen-month-old boy or girl often seems very busy just becoming. He or she is leaving lovable infancy behind and is well on the way to becoming an often difficult, certainly demanding Eighteen-month-old.

Now most are comfortably mobile in the upright position. However, they still are in every sense of the word toddlers—their balance even now is not entirely sure, though most do walk about with increasing confidence. Much as they like to walk, many still like very much to be carried. Upward extended arms and a plaintive *eh-eh* tell Mother all too plainly that heavy as they may be, they do want Mother to carry them. (And it may be only Mother who will do since this tends to be an extremely sensitive, discriminating age.)

Your typical Fifteen-month-old, though he is more able physically than earlier, is not a particularly cooperative creature. "No" definitely leads over "yes"; "won't," even though not expressed in that special word, leads over "will." The child of this age loves to empty and fill things, but admittedly most are better at dumping than at filling.

Creeping on flat surfaces is often resorted to when they are in a hurry, and most can, in their own fashion, creep up a short flight of stairs. Hands, though still not too skillful, can manage a successful tower of two small blocks.

Language in most, though still rather limited, has increased to perhaps a dozen words, and the child may be able to imitate new words spoken to him, even though he may not actually add them to his vocabulary. Many now combine two words as "See gir," "See kitty," "Were baw?" Most can respond to more words than they can verbalize, such as "Shut the door," "Bring Mommy the book."

The child of this age is beginning to want to do things

for himself, often things he really cannot quite manage. He is also very demanding—may insist on having his dish on his tray, even though he may keep throwing it to the floor. Or he may insist on having something to hold in *both* hands.

With his characteristic lack of inhibition, the Fifteen-month-old may be lost in the confusion of the living room since he tends to grab anything in sight. It works best if he can be confined to his high chair, playpen, or a large fenced-in area of the room. Motor drive, need to grab, and lack of inhibition make the child of this age at least a modest menace unless he is so restrained.

We describe the Fifteen-month-old child as demanding. But he is as demanding of himself as of others, so it may be fairer to call him assertive rather than demanding. He is asserting his budding independence. He wants to help feed himself. He grasps the cup with both hands. He boldly thrusts his spoon into his cereal and, upside down, into his mouth. (It will take almost another year before he can inhibit the turning of the spoon in this maneuver.)

The Fifteen-month-old baby is at the threshold of behavior capacities which already anticipate his behavior in nursery school and kindergarten. He can fit a round block into a round hole; he babbles in his own jargon; he gestures; he can imitate a stroke of crayon upon paper; he is no longer a mere scribbler. He can, if supervised, turn the pages of a book and may be moderately interested in being told about the pictures he sees—though admittedly he is as likely to tear the pages as to turn them carefully.

Our temptation at this time may be to press him too fast and too heavily in the direction of civilization. It is important to remember that nature requires time to organize the child's budding neuromuscular system.

EIGHTEEN MONTHS

Eighteen months is an extremely interesting halfway station between infancy and early childhood. If we as

adults are willing to respect the immaturity of the child of this age, chances are that we, and he, may experience relatively smooth sailing. If we make the mistake of thinking that just because a child is mobile and can say a few words, he is not too very different from, say, a Two-year-old, he and we both will be in trouble.

Compared to his infant self, the Eighteen-month-old can accomplish miracles. Compared to what comes after, even in a few more months, there is much that he might like to do but that is not yet within his repertoire.

The mother who said of her Eighteen-month-old, "You have to program him as if he were a robot," perhaps had it in mind that the wide variety of choice which the older child experiences is not available to the Eighteen-month-old. There is only a certain number of things he can do. He is limited in his choice of how he will behave by his very immaturities.

If it sometimes seems to parents and others in charge that your typical Eighteen-month-old is rather a difficult and hard-to-manage little person, remember, as we've said before, that things are quite as difficult for him as they may be for you. He has trouble because he cannot count on himself to do what he wants to do.

Gross Motor Behavior   Motorwise, he is starting to come into his own, but these abilities are still at an all-too-tender-stage. He can now walk upright, unaided; can even run after a fashion. But he is never safe from falling because his ability to walk is still so new. And though he walks successfully alone, he still proceeds on a very broad base, feet wide apart. Arms are sometimes flexed upward, hands at shoulders, or extended out to each side like flippers, to help with balance. The name "toddler" no doubt derives from his awkward way of walking as he bumbles around in a semibelligerent way—wide stance, head forward, abdomen sometimes protruded, mouth partly open. He can stop and start fairly well but finds it difficult to turn corners.

Walking is a bit uncertain; running, even more so. He runs with a stiff, propulsive, flat gait, looking forward, as though he were wearing blinders. And walking or running, he tends to fall suddenly, often looking as if he had just collapsed. He loves to go up and down stairs. This may be accomplished on hands and knees. When and if he walks upright, he still must use two feet to a step. Best speed is achieved in the creeping position, and some creep downstairs so fast that they almost slide, hardly touching the steps with their knees, pushing downward with their arms.

As fast as most can scoot down a flight of stairs, and as effectively as they may climb up, if in walking on a flat surface they come to a single step down, they may turn and back down rather than go forward. Similarly, though the Eighteen-month-old can seat himself on a small chair, he may still accomplish this by backing up to the chair till it touches the backs of his knees and then sitting down.

He loves to climb onto large chairs or sofas, and though this tends to be difficult, most prefer to do it by themselves, rejecting proffered help. He loves to squat and can often maintain this somewhat difficult position for a surprisingly long time.

Awkward as many may be in their coordination, there is, of course, great variation from one child to another. And actually any one child may show great unevenness of motor behavior from one situation to another. So a child who still lumbers around and bumps into things may on occasion throw up a Ping-Pong ball and successfully bat it with a paddle held in his other hand.

It has been said of the Eighteen-month-old that he almost thinks with his feet. This means simply that he does not think ahead to what he is going to do. Rather, he runs around a room almost at random, stopping to investigate briefly whatever he comes in contact with. This is in contrast with the child who moves purposefully toward an object of his choice.

When the path of a typical Eighteen-month-old during

seven minutes in a playroom is contrasted with that of the typical Two-year-old or older child (see Figure 2), one sees how much ground the Eighteen-month-old covers, almost meaninglessly or at best exploringly, compared to the older child, who spends a longer and longer time with the toy or play equipment of his choice.

In other words, the Eighteen-month-old is pure motor drive. It is almost as if one winds him up and then he functions. This means, of course, that the adult in charge must do quite a bit of his thinking for him and must not expect too much rational action from him. It also means that his attention span, though predictably a little longer than it was at Fifteen months, is still remarkably short. Do not expect him to spend any substantial length of time with any one object or on any one activity.

The child of Eighteen months not only is motor-driven but sometimes seems to be in almost constant motor activity. Watch him as he lugs, tugs, dumps, pushes, pounds, or as he moves furniture. Here he is both awkward and ambitious, and his child's chair will often get stuck in a doorway since he is not yet a good judge of space. He still cannot kick a ball, but he is able to walk into a large ball, and he can throw a small ball after a fashion.

Out for a walk he climbs onto every curbstone, explores every byway.

Gross motor activity still predominates over fine motor behavior. He can grab and push and pull, but as yet he cannot manage those fine motions of wrist and fingers which will soon make delicate manipulations a success and a pleasure.

Fine Motor Behavior　He still uses whole arm movements in ball play or in playing with a doll or toy animal. Though he does some rather wonderful things with his hands, he also is apt to fumble and drop whatever he handles. Objects by no means always do what he wants them to do. Awkwardness is shown in the fact that he is likely to pound sideways with his much-loved small rubber ham-

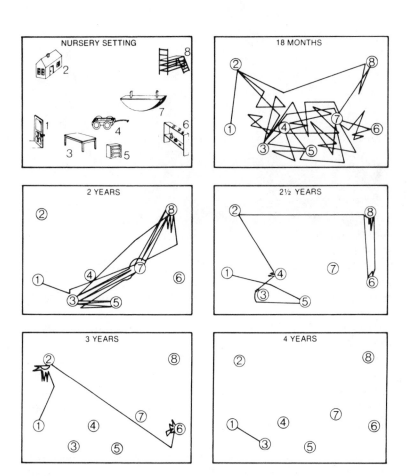

Figure 2
Seven Clocked Minutes of Nursery School
Behavior at Different Ages

mer, hitting objects with the side of his hammer, not with its head.

Hands are becoming increasingly skillful, however. Now he can turn the pages of a large picture book, though often two or three at a time. He can build a nice tower of three or four small blocks. Given paper and crayon, he can scribble spontaneously and can imitate a stroke if you show him how to make one from top to bottom of a page. He loves to pull a pull toy.

Vision The Eighteen-month-old's eyes, like his hands, can but do not always move separately from other parts of his body. Eyes alone can move up and over, over and up, or in other directions, and eye movement may precede hand or head movement. But since behavior is not as yet entirely segmented, the child will often turn his head, or even his head and whole body, as he turns his eyes.

This whole-bodiness of behavior is extremely conspicuous at this age. In fact, the child seems often to arrange his whole body at a desired distance from an object, rather than move the object toward himself. If an object is too near for comfort, the child may sit way back in his chair, then tip his head to one side or lean forward. Or he may turn his body and the chair so that his whole body is oriented toward the thing he is looking at.

There is little peripheral or sideward vision. The child seems most comfortable if he is eyeing something straight on, especially if his whole trunk is turned toward the object.

Head adjustment may substitute for eye adjustment as the child pulls in his chin and then looks out of the tops of his eyes; or thrusts his chin out and looks down his nose; or tilts his head to one side. Head and eyes move together when the child looks up. He lifts eyes and head all in one movement. Or as he puts cubes into a cup (in an examination situation), head and eyes go back and forth, back and forth, from cup to cubes (though on a rare occasion a child may keep his eyes on a pile of objects and execute quite a neat move in putting an object to one side without regard for that special object).

There is a good deal of peering: The child leans forward, thrusts chin forward, and then peers at something. Or he may lean forward and down over an object he is looking at. Occasionally a boy or girl will brush an object to the floor, or will throw it to the floor, and then look at it after it has landed.

Most at this age seem to prefer to regard objects either up close or far away. This seems more comfortable for them, as a viewing distance, than an intermediate zone. But whatever the viewing distance, there is a good deal of staring. The child is clearly taking in the world through his eyes.

Language Language at this age varies tremendously, from the talkative little girl with three or four dozen words in her vocabulary to the quiet little boy who may still be

limited to no more than half a dozen words. On the average we may expect perhaps a dozen words, including
proper names.

However, if actually counted, the number of words in
the vocabulary of a superior and talkative Eighteen-
month-old can be surprisingly large. Thus it is not unusual
for such a child to be able to say "up," "down," "oben,"
"cos," "peez," "tank you," "baby," "doggie," "Mommy,"
"Daddy," "out," "in."

In fact, even without too many words the Eighteen-
month-old has his own ways of communicating, of making
his wants known. A single syllable such as *uh-uh* or *eh-eh,*
accompanied by gesture, can tell you that he wants to be
taken up or put down or that he'd love to have a certain toy.
Most can and do *point* in such a definite and determined
way that words are not always needed, even if available.
A negative shake of the head is quite as clear a refusal as
the more customary "no."

Although the most used word, in conversation with others, does tend to be "no," the child of this age may also say
"hello" or "bye" or show and name a real or pictured object, spontaneously or in response to encouragement from
an adult. Some do not point to or name pictures, but if
asked, "Where is the doggie?" may definitely look selectively at the picture of a dog. And the child does on occasion, and if so moved, respond positively to simple, clear
verbal directions from an adult.

Language at this age seems largely egocentric. Most, of
course, do have the words "Mommy" and "Daddy" and
quite likely, if there is a baby in the family, can say
"Baby." Or they tend to know names of older siblings, and
most also know the name of the family pet.

Though most greet other family members with a smile
(if so moved), many lack names for other relatives. Most
are reasonably friendly with grandparents, but a name for
grandparents may not come along for another few
months.

The highly talkative Eighteen-month-old may not have

a great many more *words* than his less verbal brother or sister. It is more that the real talker at this age tends to use a great deal of jargon. He may babble away enthusiastically in a way that pleases him, though it does not as a rule convey a great deal of meaning to the adult.

Quite as important as the actual number of words in the vocabulary is the fact that at this age many children are beginning to combine two words into two-word sentences as "All gone," "Go ride," "Coat non," "Daddy bye," "Oh my."

A child of this age, if in a responsive mood, likes to repeat what others are doing or saying. This is especially true if an older sibling is saying something like "The dog says 'bow-wow,' " "The duck says 'quack.' " He does not, of course, repeat the entire sentence but may chime in very strongly with the "bow-wow" or "quack."

A very sensitive and sympathetic Eighteen-month-old, seeing a hurt place on somebody else's hand, may comment "Ouch!," though whether he himself is responding to the hurt or merely calling the hurt an "ouch" is, of course, not certain.

Most respond to more words than they verbalize. Most can and do, if in the mood, carry out simple errands such as fetching Daddy's slippers, Mommy's book. Many can point to eyes, nose, mouth, hair, and other body parts if asked to.

The child of this age tends to have more to say to adults than to other children. In a nursery school or day nursery situation, for instance, though perhaps silent much of the time, the Eighteen-month-old may address the *teacher* with such words as "hello," "pitty," "no," "juice," "cookie," "bye."

Different kinds of verbal interchange with a teacher may include the following:

Showing an object to her and naming it: "book," "teddy," "truck."

Commanding the teacher: "down."

Requesting something of teacher: "cookie" (or "coo"),

"water." (Or the child may, in making a request, merely point or jargon.)

Also, the child may obey a teacher's verbal request. He may defer an activity or wander away if the teacher says, "Not now."

He may repeat teacher's words "Here's John" by saying, "Ere Don."

Some combine two words or more in comment to teacher: "my choochoo," "two car," "no juice," "my get down," "see ball."

The Eighteen-month-old definitely cannot yet count on himself, when it comes to language. There is *much* he wishes to say for which he simply does not have the words. Words he does have, indeed, especially that all-important word "no," but not yet enough words to ask for all the things he wants or to explain and interpret his very strong wishes and needs. How very frustrating to want the blue bib instead of the pink one and not to have the word for "blue"! Life will be much easier in even another six months.

When the child plays either alone or in a group, a considerable amount of jargon accompanies his play. The Eighteen-month-old laughs and smiles and jabbers away as he plays by himself without necessarily directing his vocalizing to any other person. Words serve not always to communicate but seem often to be uttered for the mere pleasure of vocalization.

Adaptive and Play Behavior   The Eighteen-month-old is a busy little person. Though much of his activity is purely gross motor—bumbling around from one spot to another, climbing stairs, walking on curbs, pushing his wheel toys —hands and eyes play their parts as well. Manipulation tends to be more exploratory than skillful, but ability to handle and to combine his toys is definitely emerging.

Much of his handling of objects is admittedly still rather gross. He lugs, tugs, dumps, drags. He loves to push furniture or to pull anything on wheels; loves to fill a dish with

sand and then dump out the sand; loves to "sweep" with his little broom or to imitate other household activities.

He may play best with somewhat shapeless materials—sand, mud, clay, water. Experiments with such media can go on almost endlessly. His arms tend to work better than his hands or fingers. He is still not very skilled in fine motor adaptation.

In working a puzzle, the child may exhibit more energy than dexterity. When a child pounds with a favorite hammer, the hammer may be so aimed that its side rather than its head will strike the hammered object.

In block play the Eighteen-month-old can as a rule manage the piling of three or even four blocks, though he may not be successful every time. He tends to paint with whole arm strokes, only a few strokes to each page; he clutches a pencil or crayon in a clumsy whole-hand grasp, moving his whole arm as he marks his paper with jagged, scribbly strokes. Clay play amounts chiefly to handling and squeezing; few actual products result.

However, behavior at this age tends to be highly variable from child to child or even in any one child from time to time. In attempting to work out a simple wooden puzzle, he may merely attempt to jam a piece into a wrong place. Or he may, surprisingly, fit one corner, as the head of a bird, into its proper place and then very carefully move the rest of the piece so that it fits nicely.

Even though he does not as a rule stay long with any one activity, the typical child of this age is relatively independent. So, if in a happy mood, he can entertain himself for fairly long periods of time. He endlessly shifts from pull toy to doll to teddy bear to pots and pans to balls to blocks to hammer toy to magazines, especially those with large, colored pages. He hugs his doll one moment, drops it the next to run over and finger the light plug, then runs over to sit down and again to look at his magazine, tears out a page, gets up, and runs off to something else. Out of doors he can play for long periods, filling his pail with sand and then dumping it out.

He may become momentarily angry when things don't work his way, but his attention span is so short that this anger may not last long enough for him to call for adult help.

One of the best as well as one of the most difficult things about the child of this age is that he has such a very short attention span. This means that it is sometimes hard to keep him entertained since his interest shifts so quickly. But it also means that he quickly forgets his objection to some activity which is giving trouble.

If the adult's idea of what would be fun to play with happens to fit his (say you offer a pegboard the pegs of which can be hammered into their proper holes with his favorite hammer), the child of this age may take his clues from the adult. But if your suggestion does not meet with his momentary whim, he tends to go his way and let you go yours.

Some rather advanced Eighteen-month-olds can be intrigued momentarily into letting you "read" to them or at least show them pictures in a book and talk about them. For most, book interest is nowhere near as long or as strong as it will be in even another six months.

Television watching, too, a highly favored activity of the older preschooler, is not a great favorite of most Eighteen-month-olds. Any attention they may give to the screen tends to be extremely fleeting. Some like the movement and flash of color. It is unlikely that they are greatly intrigued by the plot.

Music has a varying appeal. Some will listen briefly, especially to a child's phonograph. Others do not seem to care very much for music.

And whatever their interest, in spite of occasional rather long periods of concentration on some favorite activity, most play with any single object or set of objects tends to be fleeting. A lick and a promise and then on to something else.

TWENTY-ONE MONTHS

Almost suddenly in many, as they move on from the egocentricity and self-involvement of Eighteen months to the often surprising outgoingness and maturity of Two years of age, come new adaptive abilities. In some rather advanced boys and girls these changes begin clearly around Twenty-one months of age. In others, they do not make their appearance till the child is well into Two.

One of the most conspicuous and rather delightful of these changes is an interest in and ability to distinguish ownership of objects. Many Twenty-one-month-olds seem almost suddenly highly aware of what belongs to whom. Many seem quite clear about which objects belong to which members of the family. The typical Eighteen-month-old cares chiefly about what is "mine." The Twenty-one-month-old can care about what is "yours."

So a child of this age can say specifically, "This is Mommy's," or, "Where Bobby's book?" This, of course, occurs at home. In a store, a child of this age may, if not prevented, walk off with anything within reach.

Also, many now have a rather good idea of where household objects belong and like to put them in their places. For example, the child may be able to put the silver away as Mother wipes the dishes or may help Mother unpack after a vacation. He will take an armful of clothes and, on direction, *may* put them where they belong.

With or even sometimes without demonstration, a child of this age can fit circular rings of varying sizes into each other to make a full circle. If he puts in a ring that is too small, he can take it out and insert one of the proper next size.

One little girl was observed holding a cracker in her hand and picking up a package of her father's cigarettes in the other. By accident, she dropped one cigarette. She then tried to put the package in the same hand with her

41

cracker in order to pick up the dropped cigarette. Failing, she tucked the package between her forearm and body and then picked up the cigarette from the floor.

In other words, instead of merely looking for help, as earlier, this child can now solve certain problems for herself.

So far as language goes, it is important to keep clearly in mind that girls in general talk sooner and talk much more fluently than do boys. Many boys, even at Twenty-one months, may still speak chiefly in one- or at most two-word sentences. Many still may be jargoning. Others will still use pointing and *eh-eh* as perhaps their chief means of communication.

In contrast, a well-endowed little girl of Twenty-one months may already speak in short sentences, even though still with infantile pronunciation. Thus, when mittens are being put on her, she may say "zum [thumb] in ere, pees." Or, "Ere Daddy, maggie [magazine]." Or "Bing, Mommy, bing [play the piano]."

She may even like to practice language. For instance, if asked to put a letter into her mother's hand, she may say repeatedly, "Into, into," giving the letter over and over to her mother. But either boys or girls may stand, rigid and frozen, if they don't have the words they need and thus cannot make their wants known.

In general, then, Twenty-one months tends to be one of those slippery, somewhat unpredictable ages. At times the boy or girl slips back to the egocentric, demanding, oppositional, and hard-to-get-along-with level of the Eighteen-month-old. Then, at other times, the child shows delightful glimpses of the smooth, friendly, relatively mature little person he or she will become by the second birthday. Your Twenty-one-month-old can be a constant surprise.

chapter five
THE CHILD
WITH OTHER PEOPLE

Your typical Fifteen-month-old is not primarily a people person. Except that they take care of his many needs—especially as they push him in his carriage—he could pretty well do without them.

He does as a rule accept his mother's help in the daily routines—eating, dressing, bathing—though even here he tends either to take help for granted or to resist bitterly. As we've said before, he is not always an easy fellow to get along with.

On his favorite carriage ride he pays virtually no attention to the person pushing him, beyond expressing displeasure if the ride should come to a halt for even a minute.

With other children, he for the most part pays very little attention to those about him, except that he may grab for whatever they may be playing with or perhaps push them out of the way.

Some Fifteen-month-olds are so asocial that they will not even accept something, say, a cracker, directly from the hand of the adult. They would much prefer to take it from a dish.

Though many at this age treat their caretakers more or less as part of the furniture, they are not without personal charm. Caught in a tender moment, they may go back to

their earlier baby ways. So when they are in a very good mood, they may perform their earlier delightful tricks— wave bye-bye, play pat-a-cake, respond to "Where's the baby?" They may even accept a proffered caress.

But for the most part the boy or girl of this age tends to be independent, undemonstrative, concerned more with his or her own needs and wishes than with those of some other person whether child or adult.

Even more than the Fifteen-month-old, your typical Eighteen- to Twenty-one-month-old is a young person of almost unbelievable egocentricity. He is almost all "take," almost no "give." He wants what he wants, and he wants it now. He has very little wish to please or to do

something just because somebody else wants him to.

He is so extremely self-centered that much of the time he does not relate to another person even when asking something of that person. So, if he wishes to be picked up after his nap, he may characteristically express this wish by holding up his arms. He may even supplement this gesture by flexing and extending his fingers repeatedly. But one feels that he might make this gesture to anyone available, not just to you in particular.

Similarly, if you take him for a long stroller ride, it seems not a specially sociable occasion. So far as one can tell, a motor attached to his stroller to keep it going might do quite as well as mother, grandmother, or baby-sitter.

For the most part adults appear to exist, in his mind, solely to carry out his wishes and demands. Thus his social behavior consists mostly of his making demands of other people, by either word or gesture. One of his most trying demands occurs when he is feeling dependent and unhappy. Then his constant "Up, up," addressed to Mother, can become extremely wearing.

With most grown-ups, in fact, he is less fun than he used to be. Just earlier he may have enjoyed being rocked and sung to. He liked to hear that "Mommy [Daddy, Grammy, whoever] is rocking Bobby." Now, even if you capture him, he tends to straighten out and slide out of your lap. Many are so unsharing, of themselves and of their possessions, that they will not even let you put your hand on the arms of their chairs.

And, as mentioned earlier, it is extremely difficult for the child of this age to adapt his actions to your demands.

However, there is no question but that the child of this age relates to adults better than he does to other children. He does turn to his mother when in trouble or even sometimes when tired. He may on rare occasion show affection. And he enjoys roughhousing with his father, though he may refuse to let his father feed or change him. And it is definitely Mother he wants if he is in trouble.

The girl or boy sometimes responds to a verbal "no, no" or to directions given in simple single words as "coat," "hat," "out."

Though he can by no means be considered a help around the house, the child of this age may like to mimic such household activities as sweeping or dusting. He does relate possessions to their owners and may even like to fetch things (as Father's slippers). He can also go to places where things are kept and ask for them, if they are out of reach, by pointing and saying *eh-eh.*

EIGHTEEN TO TWENTY-ONE MONTHS

A charting of children in the nursery school situation (Figure 3) shows that the Eighteen- to Twenty-one-month-old talks most to himself, a jargon type of verbalization

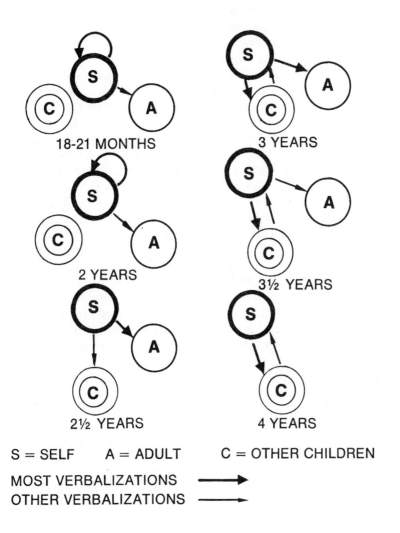

18-21 MONTHS

3 YEARS

2 YEARS

3½ YEARS

2½ YEARS

4 YEARS

S = SELF   A = ADULT   C = OTHER CHILDREN

MOST VERBALIZATIONS ⟶

OTHER VERBALIZATIONS ⟶

Figure 3
Person to Whom the Child Talks Most

often accompanying his solitary play. The next largest number of comments are made to a teacher. There is virtually no comment addressed to other children.

In any school situation the child of this age will need close and constant supervision by an adult.

Though he may on occasion be somewhat responsive to his parents or other adults, the typical Eighteen- to Twenty-one-month-old is not yet much interested in other children, at home or outside. To a large extent he ignores them or treats them as objects, poking at their eyes or pulling at their hair—not so much in anger or hostility as by way of exploration. He may grab an object from another child with little attention to the child grabbed from.

In general he tends to treat other children as if they were furniture or other objects. He may bump into them, walk over them, poke at them. He seems to have little notion that he may be hurting the other child by his inquisitiveness or rough treatment. Actually he may be quite as destructive of other children as of objects since he makes small distinction between animate and inanimate.

If he is playing in a group, except for fights over objects or an often rough inspection of some other child, his play is largely solitary. Most children at this age do not even play for long beside another child, as they will do as Two years of age approaches. For the most part in any group situation, children remain extremely isolated. Three or more may play in separate parts of a room not even looking in each other's direction. They tend to act as if alone in a room. Or they may just crowd into the space already occupied by another child. If one child looks at another, it tends to be with a rather blank stare.

The typical Eighteen-month-old does not as a rule even stand beside another child, though he may stand beside a teacher. By Twenty-one months several may group together around a teacher. Not until they are about Two, as a rule, do two children stand or play side by side. And even here this is not the customary alignment.

Any verbalization tends to be less than social: "No," "Go way," or *eh-eh* if he wants something held by another child.

The majority, though seemingly most content with solitary play, do pay more attention to the teacher, or other adults, than to other children. A child may ignore the teacher, even visually, or may grab something from her without regard or comment. However, he may approach her to show her something and may comment as he does so: "block" or "car." Or he may respond to her comment that another boy is named John by saying, "E Don."

He may imitate some action or gesture of the teacher's, though if a teacher starts putting pegs into a pegboard and then hands a peg to a child, the child may merely hold out his peg to the teacher, rather than imitate her insertion of the peg into the board.

If asking for help, a child may simply squeal or babble to the teacher. If he does not want to do what she wants him to he may just shake his head or say "no."

Children do accept proffered physical help from a teacher or day care worker as they would from their mother, though this is not particularly personal. They may accept an offered helping hand without glance or comment. Or they may fall off high places into the teacher's arms with an automatic assumption that they will be caught.

Eighteen- to Twenty-one-month-olds may like to look at a younger sibling but beyond that do not as a rule pay much attention to him. They may or may not be jealous, depending on temperament and circumstance.

The child of this age learns a tremendous amount from those just older because of his imitative qualities. Thus, if a brother or sister tells him, "Doug, say 'moo,' " or "Doug, say 'quack-quack!',", or in an excess of good manners, "Say 'Thanks, Mom,' " he will obligingly say "moo," "quack-quack," or "Thanks, Mom." This kind of imitation undoubtedly helps speed up verbalization or at least increase its quantity.

However, if he is playing with a sibling very near his age and the two start fighting, it may be almost impossible to separate them. A jump rope which neither really wants can be lying idle till one grabs it. Then the other suddenly wants it, too, and a real tug-of-war ensues. Physically removing either the jump rope or the children may be your only recourse. The problem usually cannot be solved in a logical or reasonable manner.

Grandparents may be the ones who are most disappointed in the characteristic self-centeredness and (often) lack of warmth in response to the approaches of other people of the child of this age. Just younger, the boy or girl

would often cuddle with, laugh with, and respond affectionately to others. Now he or she may remain quite indifferent, even staring at you blankly if you approach with too great enthusiasm.

It is extremely important for grandparents, especially those who do not see the child on a regular basis, to appreciate that this indifference and lack of responsiveness will in all likelihood be rather temporary. Even by the time the child is Two years of age, his or her earlier much appreciated warmth and friendliness will very probably have returned.

A few may respond positively to almost anybody. Others seem to make a fairly clear distinction between people known to them and strangers. But even with friends and family, their response is not consistently friendly.

It's fair to say that for the child, whether boy or girl, the second half of the second year of life is a bewildering age. Each child meets the age and meets other people in his or her own special way. Some attack. As one mother put it, "He puts all the strength he has into his 'No!'" Others throw tantrums when their unspoken wants and needs are not met. Others withdraw and face you with a stony or sad stare. This is a poor age for communication between adult and child, but each child does make it in his or her own fascinating and special way.

chapter six
ROUTINES

Twelve to Fifteen Months The earlier two naps a day have now given way in many to merely a morning nap, though by Fifteen months this one nap a day may have moved to after lunch. Many sleep for as much as two hours. They accept this nap without objection, and most fall asleep right away.

Bedtime comes between 6:00 and 8:00 P.M. As with the nap, most accept this without question and fall asleep quickly. Some do, some do not, wake in the night and cry for someone to come to them. Morning waking comes between 6:00 and 8:00.

Eighteen to Twenty-one Months Sleeping for many at this age is an easy routine. The daily nap is still very important and is usually a taken-for-granted part of the child's day. It usually takes place after lunch. The child may or may not take toys to bed with him, but he is often so ready for bed that he goes right to sleep. His nap may last for one and a half to two hours. He usually wakes happy, though wet, and is ready to get right up. Toileting follows nap.

Bedtime continues to be somewhere between 6:00 and

8:00 P.M. and is usually well accepted. Bedtime demands and stalling have not yet made their appearance in most. The child may play with his teddy bear or other stuffed toy or doll briefly before dropping off to sleep. However, by Twenty-one months some do have difficulty going to sleep. Now begins the calling parent back after the child is seemingly settled down. Also, night sleep may be more disturbed than earlier, even in a normally good sleeper.

Some do wake during the night, but as a rule they are rather easily quieted. The time of morning waking, like bedtime, is rather variable. Most still wake somewhere between 6:00 and 8:00 A.M. They may lie quietly for a while and then, when ready to get up, call their parents. Or they may wake, call for a bottle or something to eat, and then go back to sleep. Most enjoy a rather good night's sleep of often as much as twelve hours, with or without night waking. Since their daytimes tend to be extremely active, most need this good long night's rest.

FEEDING

Twelve to Fifteen Months   The majority of breast-fed babies are off the breast by this time. Three meals are now for most the order of the day. At Twelve months the gross motor drive may be so great that one may need to allow the child to stand as he or she is being fed. Most are willing to be fed, especially if they have a toy or toys to play with, and will open their mouths as the food approaches. By Fifteen months they may be better at remaining seated during the meal, but a drive to feed oneself may be coming in so that mealtime may be messier than it was earlier. More food gets into their mouths when they finger-feed than when they try to manipulate the spoon.

Eighteen to Twenty-one Months   The robust infant appetite may already be decreasing, and the child does not necessarily eat three "good" meals a day. Now that he has shifted from breast or bottle to cup, less milk is drunk.

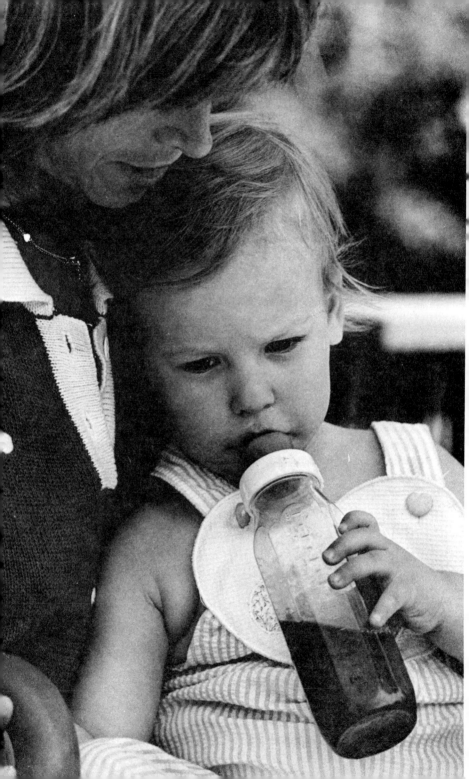

Appetite for milk from a cup is usually less than appetite for milk from a bottle. Thus some mothers prefer to continue with one bottle a day. (Or the child himself hangs on to his bottle, at least part time.)

Your Eighteen-month-old still tends to be rather accepting of the type of food that is offered, even though he may not consume as much as Mother thinks he ought to. But by Twenty-one months special preferences and refusals of certain foods may be extremely strong and should be respected.

The child now tries hard to manage his own spoon. Grasp of the spoon is pronate. The Eighteen- to Twenty-one-month-old holds his spoon horizontally, raising his elbow as he lifts spoon to mouth. The spoon is aligned to the mouth and may turn as it enters the mouth. The child's free hand is ready to help as needed, and it often is needed, to push food on the lips into the mouth or to place spilled food on the spoon.

The child may even carry food from his dish with his fingers and place it in the spoon bowl (or at least touch it to the spoon bowl) just before putting spoon (or food) into his mouth. Some foods he prefers to finger-feed.

Most can manage their own cups with rather little spilling. The hazard in cup drinking is that when the child has finished his drink, he automatically extends his cup to his mother. If she is not there to catch it, he is apt to drop it onto the floor.

The child of this age enjoys feeding himself, though Mother needs to be near in case small problems arise. Feeding now may be for nourishment. Or it may be just for fun. Thus a child may pound a peg through his sandwich, may stuff his sandwich into his mouth, or may just crumble it. Food is likely to end up either all over his face or all over the floor. Mealtime is indeed messy.

This second half of the first year may seem early, indeed, to be thinking about feeding your child a proper diet. It may seem to you that just getting the food into him or her is quite enough. Not so. It is never too early to think about

what kinds of foods you are giving your child. Breast feeding will, of course, give any infant the very best nutritional start possible. But clearly your concern does not stop once he or she is weaned from the breast.

We recommend that any mother of a preschooler, no matter how young, consult *The Taming of the C.A.N.D.Y. Monster* by Vicki Lansky and *Feed Your Kids Right* by Dr. Lendon Smith. These and other useful books on nutrition do point out that it is never too early to give serious consideration to what you are feeding your children.

It is no longer considered enough just to give a child a "good balanced diet," though this, of course, is primary. It is also important to avoid additives and preservatives and any so-called junk foods and to cut back on salt and fat.

Substitute poultry and fish for beef. Do all you can to prevent your child from developing a taste for sugar.

These are general rules. Each child tends to have his or her own particular food idiosyncrasies. Many children behave as if their bodies were in chemical warfare. They respond adversely to foods which other members of the family may take in their stride. Even as young as Eighteen to Twenty-one months of age, if your child is chronically cranky, unhappy, irritable, you should at least consider the possibility that something he eats is doing him actual harm.

More than this, it would be wise to consider the possibility that your child needs vitamins other than those provided by even the best of diets. A competent allergist or nutritionist can be of great help to you in setting up and maintaining a diet which not only will agree with your child but can be one of the biggest helps you could provide in keeping him not only healthy but happy.

ELIMINATION

Twelve to Fifteen Months The Twelve-month-old may respond to being placed on a potty for his bowel movement, but successes may actually be fewer than just earlier. By Fifteen months children may be better about accepting and responding to placement on the potty, and many are fairly consistently successfully trained for their BMs.

Many, though by no means all, are now dry when they wake from their naps and thus it is often possible to "catch" them and to encourage successful urination on the potty at this time of day. Some respond favorably to being put on the toilet at certain times, as after meals or after any sleeping period.

However, some either defecate or urinate only just *after* they are taken off the toilet. (And some do not even make this relationship.) Successes should be accepted with moderate enthusiasm when they occur, but any formal efforts at consistent toilet training should, of course, not be pushed at this time.

Eighteen to Twenty-one Months   Toileting at this age may be more of a problem than earlier since some mothers are now beginning to look forward to a time when the child may take increasing responsibility. With most, there is still a long, long way to go.

Children vary a great deal in the timing of their bowel movements. Any one child may have a mealtime relationship for a time and then may shift to midmorning or mid-afternoon. This shift in timing makes successful training difficult. Many now do request the toilet with a word or gesture or by fetching their potty. Or often a mother can judge by the child's unusual quietness that he or she is about to function.

Those children who have a meal association are usually trained more easily than those who do not. There may be two daily movements, one after breakfast and one after supper. The early talker who has a word for this function is perhaps trained more quickly than the child without such a word.

Children who have an irregular time of functioning commonly have their movements when alone, often in the midmorning, and often when they are standing at their playpens or crib rails. They usually want to be changed. Such children usually resist the toilet and may even have occasional episodes of stool smearing. Tightly fastened diapers can help prevent this unattractive but basically harmless behavior.

As to bladder functioning, most do not object to being put on the toilet at this age if they are not put on too often and if Mother does not make too much of a fuss. The child may even ask for toileting with some such sound as *uh-uh* and may shake his head yes or no when asked if he wants to go. This, however, would represent rather advanced behavior at this age.

Many still seem quite oblivious to the whole thing. And though some may now notice the puddles they make, many others do not. If the child does notice puddles or dampness, it may be a sign that he may soon be ready for serious training. If he or she remains totally unaware, success at staying dry is still a long way off. And Mother might do best to hold off on any efforts at training. Toilet training begun too early does not bring results other than increasing resistance, so it should be avoided. Better to wait too long to begin than to rush in and try to push a child to dryness for which he or she is in no way ready.

BATH AND DRESSING

Twelve to Fifteen Months   With a Twelve-month-old the bath, which is usually very much enjoyed, comes at any time of day that is convenient for the parent. By Fifteen months, since the nap is usually in the afternoon, the bath may fit in best at bedtime. The child of this age may try to suck water from the washcloth or to put the washcloth on his head or may fool around with his water toys, but he or she tends to enjoy the bath and to be reasonably easy to handle.

The Twelve-month-old is also usually quite easy to dress —giving little difficulty. By Fifteen months dressing may be more difficult. The child's attention is usually on other things. Thus the parent needs to hold the child tightly and more or less pour him into his clothes.

Eighteen to Twenty-one Months   Though now the bath is often given just before bedtime, if your child is stimulated rather than relaxed by his bath, it should be moved to an earlier hour. Most accept their bath happily, though some, if they have fallen in the tub or been afraid of the sound of water going down the drain, may temporarily object. A rubber mat placed on the bottom of the tub may help give such children a feeling of security.

Dressing is usually not too great a problem. Some now

make a big fuss at having their diapers changed. Such children are often calmed and made more cooperative by being given a chance to participate in the changing. A nice game of "pin please," in which the child is allowed to hold, and at the proper time hand to Mother, a large diaper pin, may solve the problem of trying to diaper a struggling child. (This, of course, applies best to diapers that are fastened with pins, though even with those which are taped, an unnecessary pin can be brought in as an accessory, to ensure cooperation.)

The child of this age is becoming interested in the process of being dressed and may be quite cooperative. He may even be able to fetch his own shoes and put them on, though often on the wrong feet. Most are, however, better at undressing than at dressing. Many can remove mittens, hats, socks and even unzip zippers.

With their special skill at undressing, some at this age take off all their clothes and, unless watched closely, may then run around the house or even the yard stark naked. They seem to enjoy the freedom that nudity brings. If you or your neighbors object to this, dress your child in garments which are hard to remove or have fastenings in the back. Even take a big stitch or two if you have to.

Awareness of the connection between outdoor clothing and outdoor activity is often shown by the fact that when an adult suggests going out for a walk, the child may either fetch hat or coat or ask, "Were coat?" He or she may also show awareness that at least certain garments (especially slippers) belong to certain members of the family.

chapter seven
TECHNIQUES

Techniques most effective as your One-year-old moves into the Fifteen- to Twenty-one-month age zone tend to be unique, quite different from those we use at any other age.

When your child is still a mere Twelve-month-old, you as a parent may not think of your ways of handling as techniques. You bathe your baby, dress him, feed him, play with him, enjoy him. Some babies are easier to manage than others, but most, if normal and healthy, enjoy attention paid to them and respond positively. Since to a large extent you do still have rather much the upper hand —a baby is somewhat at your tender mercy—you do not have to think of ways of getting around him.

Also, at least to a large extent, we try to *satisfy* babies. Baby demands; we provide. He cries, and we hasten to find out why—is he hungry, wet, lonely, too hot or too cold, or in some specific discomfort?

True, even in infancy, especially as the baby begins to be mobile and starts getting into things, there are a few no-no's. And even with a self-demand feeding schedule (baby is fed when hungry rather than at set and certain times), we think not just of self-demand but also of self-regulation. That is, we do not feed him *every* time he cries. He gradually learns to wait a little.

And though we do not always think of it this way, disci-

pline does begin in infancy. The infant learns, rather early, from the world around him what things work, what are permitted. But still, it would be fair to say that most of us do not think much about using techniques with our infants.

As the child becomes more of a person, the situation changes. True, you are still larger and stronger, but if he doesn't want to do what you choose to have him do, by Fifteen or Eighteen months he can make a very substantial fuss. It becomes increasingly difficult to manage him when your will and his collide.

Yet the usual child in this age range is not yet ready for

those customary life-saving, face-saving preschool techniques which will make living more possible when he is slightly older. Not for him such hopeful suggestions as "How about?," "Let's," "Shall we?," "Where do the red ones go?"

Discipline, to a very large extent, at this time is not a matter of deciding what you want your child to do and then seeing to it that he or she complies. Rather, it is a matter of thinking largely in terms of what he or she is able to do—both physically able and emotionally able—and then seeing to it that your demands fall within the limits of these abilities.

That is, you do use techniques—but techniques suited to the age and personality of your individual girl or boy. Possibly the biggest error which parents make with the child of this age is in thinking of him as more capable than he really is or in deciding that it is time for him to *mind.*

Now that he is mobile and talking, some parents assume that they need merely to tell their child to "Come here, dear" and he will, or should, do just that. Not so, as experience will show you. And so it is that you introduce techniques. If you are wise, your handling will be suited to the child's immaturity.

If your techniques are extremely skillful and if you are fortunate to have a rather adaptable child, chances are you can get him to do what you want him to possibly more than half the time. But there are times, even with a good-natured child, that even your best techniques may not succeed.

Specific suggestions as to techniques which one hopes may work will be discussed here in two separate sections —Fifteen to Eighteen months and Eighteen to Twenty-one months—though inevitably there will be considerable overlap. Many of the things which we shall suggest may be quite useful through this entire, often difficult year of life.

FIFTEEN TO EIGHTEEN MONTHS

At this time, just before "real" language comes in, any child tends to have a great deal of difficulty. His wants and needs are strong, but he cannot verbalize most of them. Therefore, he tends to grab and cry and scream. Tantrums may be his way of expressing his frustrations caused by the fact that there is so much he wants but cannot have, so many things he does or wants to do that are definite no-no's.

So try your best to be a flexible and ingenious guesser as to what it is that he does want. Fortunately some children at this age are rather easily distracted so that a new and interesting object if offered may prove to be a satisfactory substitute for the thing he really wanted. Or a total change of scene (lifting the child up and putting him somewhere else) may help him forget his frustration.

Not only is language not much help at this age, but fine motor coordination is often rather sketchy. Thus the child may not yet be interested in spending long periods sitting quietly and playing nicely with his toys, as he may just later on.

Gross motor activity may be his best outlet. Fortunately many children do not have to be actually moving themselves. They may be quite content with long car or carriage rides. A child who can be extremely difficult at home will often sit still for a good hour or more while being wheeled in his stroller. So take full advantage of the child's love of motion.

Personal-social relations may not be too useful at this time in making or keeping boy or girl happy. Whereas earlier this child may have been passively content to cuddle or to be rocked or sung to, now he is too active to accept what may seem to him like restraint. So a toddler gym, or doorway swing, or any object which permits almost constant motion, with it is hoped little danger to himself or others, can be a very, very useful thing.

Children of this age love to swing or to bounce up and down.

Often, as an interest in books and pictures dawns, picture books become meaningful. Something as simple as *Pat the Bunny* may keep a child happily occupied for ten or fifteen minutes at a time.

Pounding toys or a xylophone (which, of course, can also be pounded) can be a tremendous success.

As to his daily routines try to be as flexible as possible. When any routine seems to be giving special trouble, you may save time by interrupting what you are doing, briefly, and then returning to it once the child has forgotten his objection.

When it comes to feeding, let him do as much as he can and will. Just put something under his chair so that you won't worry that he is spilling, and let it go at that. Don't worry either about the amount of food spilled or the amount eaten. Few starve themselves.

And in general, as you will need to do also at Eighteen to Twenty-one months, try to force yourself not to be too much influenced or affected by inevitable crying spells and tantrums. The less they bother you, chances are the less frequently they will occur. It is not much satisfaction to play to an uninterested audience.

Some children at this age become rather clinging and do not want to let their mothers out of their sight. If your child wails unduly when you leave the house or the room, and if your departure is necessary, just proceed. As a rule, any grief and anxiety expressed when Mommy moves out of sight tends to be rather brief. If you are leaving the house, see that he is busy with the baby-sitter before you slip out. The sitter can later reassure him, when he realizes his mother has gone, that she will be back soon.

In short, do what you reasonably can to keep life comfortable for your son or daughter, but try not to be too much upset or surprised when all does not go smoothly.

EIGHTEEN TO TWENTY-ONE MONTHS

The Eighteen- to Twenty-one-month-old is easily frustrated and at his worst may simply throw himself onto the floor and kick and scream, no matter what you do. In such cases, it is perhaps best either to remove the child from the room or even simpler, if you are reasonably sure he won't harm himself substantially, to remove yourself from the room and wait till the storm is over.

A full-fledged tantrum is the child's way of telling you when things go wrong or when he or she has had enough. Most parents find that the very best way to combat a tantrum is, so far as possible, to ignore it. Better still is to know your child and the limits of his endurance well enough so that to a large extent you can divert or support him when things are going just too wrong, so that you can prevent the tantrum before it occurs.

In fact, one of your very best possible techniques, if a tantrum threatens, is distraction. Let's say you are putting your toddler into his high chair at mealtime and he stiffens out and refuses to fit into the chair and then goes on to wave his arms and scream. Do not continue stuffing him into the chair. Instead, give up this project for the moment. Let him get down onto the floor and then distract him in some interesting way.

You might let him go to the refrigerator and select some bit of food that looks good to him. Or you might clown around and get him to join you in a dance or jig. Do anything which gets him into good humor and makes him forget that he did not want to sit in his chair and have lunch. Then a second attempt, without any special emphasis on what you are doing, may be met with no opposition at all.

(And so far as food goes, you will save yourself much pushing and shoving and coaxing and demanding by respecting the limits of the child's own appetite. Remember that if he gets one good solid meal a day, in addition to two snack types of meal, the likelihood is that he will get all the food he needs.)

Whatever the problem, you may find that distraction is your most effective secret weapon. Attention span is so very short at this age that many children will go from tears to laughter if an interesting distraction can be offered.

However, if you don't have time for, or are not in the mood for, distraction, you might try simply ignoring any tantrum that may arise. Even a very young child tends not to carry on unduly if there is absolutely no audience.

And don't feel that if you did everything just "right," there would be no tantrums, no fussing, no crying and no carrying-on. As one experienced mother remarked calmly when her Eighteen-month-old had clearly reached the point where nothing, but nothing, would please him, "He's just having his fussies."

Fatigue can be one of the outstanding reasons for these "fussies," and it is extremely important to recognize signs of fatigue, both in yourself and in your child. Frustrations easily withstood when he is rested loom large when he is tired. Bad behavior which you yourself can stand when you are rested can become a bone of vast contention if you are tired. We have no guaranteed recipe for preventing fatigue, but it is important to recognize it in both yourself and your child.

It is best, of course, if and when you can, to set things up so that tears and tantrums do not occur. You will avoid disappointment on your part and frustration on his by good evaluation of your child's inabilities and immaturities. Discovering that he does indeed walk down a one-way street and that the street tends to go in a direction other than the one you have in mind, you will not rely too much on simple directions as the customary "Come here, dear." If you need to have the child where you are, there are several good ways of getting him there if you but reckon with his immaturity.

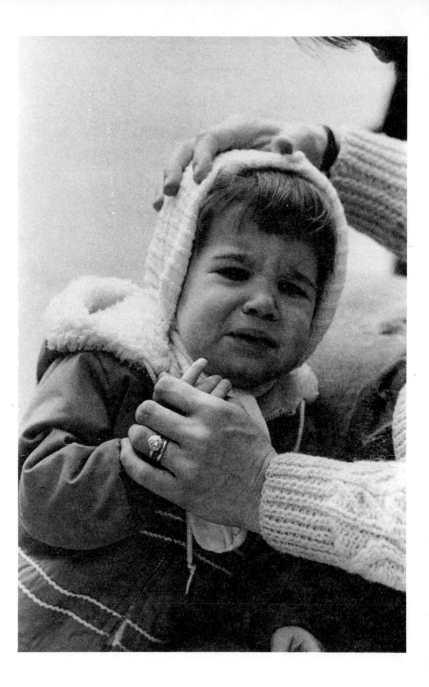

You *can* go up behind him, lift him up, and move him to where you want him to be. You will get farther with the child of this age by lifting him bodily and putting him where you want him to be than by talking to him. Or you can hold out a beloved toy, or cookie, or any other enticing object. Or you can turn your back to him and crackle a piece of paper or make some other interesting noise. Chances are he will come to find out what it is that you are doing. There are many indirect ways to persuade your child to do what you want him to. Just try to discover the stimulus that will attract—and there are many.

Perhaps your very best clue to the management of the child in this middle part of the second year of life is *not* to expect him to do things to please you. Do expect him to do things to please himself. Knowing your own child, you can rather easily discover those things which are interesting to him, those things which he likes to do, those things which will lure him from one place to another.

For the child who loves outdoors, just the word "out" may be all that is needed. Or if he associates his hat with a walk outdoors, you can say the word "hat" or produce it. In fact, at all times very simple language will be your best bet. Do not confuse your boy or girl with words that are too big.

Once outdoors, he may bumble into every byway, want to pick up every fallen twig. Remember that *everything* is new to and interesting to the child of this age. Urging him to hurry is not a good motivator. Walking away from him backward for some reason or other makes you attractive to him, and the chances are he will come running.

Out of doors one of your best techniques is to put him into his stroller and then to go for a long, long walk. Most boys and girls at this age *love* carriage rides. This is not an interpersonal activity, as we point out elsewhere, even though you will be doing the pushing. What the child seems to enjoy is the activity, the variety of scene, the motion. Many, even the most difficult and least easily satisfied, will ride contentedly as long as anyone is available to push them. Similarly many are equally content to go for long car rides.

In fact, since the out-of-doors often offers more opportunities and fewer hazards than does indoors, spend as much time as you can outside the house.

Your Eighteen- to Twenty-one-month-old may very likely resist being touched or having his arm held (even when he darts dangerously out into the street), but many will accept a harness if it is used only when needed. The harness should be used with loose reins except when needed. The reins can be looped up when not in use.

The child of this age not only may resist being touched but may not even permit you to touch the arm of the chair in which he is sitting. He tends to hit at you or at your hand. It is very important not to take this personally, not to feel rejected and to react accordingly. Rather, accept the fact that the child is just protecting his turf. Take your hand away and either apologize or just ignore the entire incident, and in the future give him more living space.

Inside, the success of the child's play depends largely upon the *presence* of multiple, even though simple, playthings and the *absence* of any hazardous equipment. Because the child of this age is a furniture mover and is beginning to be a good climber, it is wise to remove chests of drawers and small tables and chairs which he can move, while he is playing in his room. If a chest of drawers remains, the drawers should be locked to keep him from getting into them. Or his dresser *could* be turned to face the wall. Windows and screens should, of course, be securely fastened.

Toys which are too difficult to handle, and which thus bring on crying, or toys which offer any hazard whatever should be permitted only when adults are present. Books which the child is likely to tear should not be left available, even though you may be willing for him to play with (and tear) discarded magazines. Light plugs should be either disconnected or covered over because of the danger of

an electric shock resulting from the child's inserting sharp metal objects.

Valuable or breakable objects of your own should so far as possible be removed from reach. This is not the age to teach the child to *mind* or to *leave things alone.* Much less energy will be required, and much greater success achieved in this direction, when he is quite a bit older. At this time you will merely end up frustrated and unsuccessful.

Actually one of your very best techniques at this age, as it will be for some time to come, is to provide gates or other barriers which, without your saying anything, will keep the child out of areas of the house which offer danger to child or property. So one of your very best bets is to have plenty of small folding gates. A gate on the bedroom door is very useful, as is one at the top or bottom of the stairs. A gate should shut off the kitchen except when you can be there with him.

The bathroom must definitely be kept out of bounds, either by use of a gate or by locking the door. It is not just that the medicine chest must of course, be locked and fully out of reach. But toilet paper can be pulled out endlessly if the child is not prevented. And most love to throw things down the toilet bowl.

As mentioned above, when the child is in motion, especially out of doors or in a public place, a nice little harness, which can be looped up when not needed, provides a wonderfully useful extension to your own arm.

Sometimes, when the child realizes that he is taking something he shouldn't, he will run away and drop the object as he runs. Do not make an issue of it.

This is not the age at which you will successfully decide, "It's high time now that he does so-and-so." High time or not, if his body and brain are not ready, you are not likely to succeed. Great patience and a wise assessment of what he or she *is* ready for will save you a great deal of time and trouble.

Discipline as we usually think of it is not the important thing at this age. It is not necessary yet to make the child *obey* you in the conventional sense. It is more important, by whatever means you can, to arrange just to get him smoothly through the day.

In general, you will see that the chief techniques effective with a Fifteen- to Twenty-one-month-old are rather gross and physical. You control him by controlling the surroundings and by just not having too many things around that will get him into difficulty. Or you control his activity by a harness or simply by picking him up and putting him where you want him to be, without words and with no big fuss.

Language in general is not (as it will be later) his strongest motivator. If you do use language to motivate him, keep it very simple, and use words of one syllable only. And remember the mother's comment "You program him as if he were a robot." This was said not unfeelingly, just in full appreciation of the child's basic immaturities.

One of the best techniques, if one thinks of it as such, is to permit without comment any of the usual tensional outlets which give so much support and comfort to the child of this age. He sucks his thumb. (This may go on for as much as several hours a day as well as before sleep or even during sleep.) Permit it. He drags around his much-loved security blanket. So be it. He seeks the solace of a pacifier. Unless you have strong personal feelings against it, this, too, can be allowed. He still clings to his bottle. Though it is not desirable for a child to go to bed sucking at some sweet liquid, most parents do permit a comforting bottle if the child wants it. Whatever gives comfort is worth its weight in gold.

In fact, naps, though they may not be usually thought of as such, can be one of your best techniques. They free you from the child, and they free him from the demands of his own busyness and exertion.

So far as you reasonably can, plan your day around his

schedule. This works much better than trying to live as you did before he came, just fitting him into *your* day.

One final thing which a parent might keep in mind at this or any other age: This is that much cranky, irritable behavior can be due to the child's allergic reaction to something he is eating, drinking, or inhaling. A visit to a good pediatric allergist is never a mistake if your child seems to be continually unhappy and nothing you try either pleases or satisfies him.

chapter eight
MENTAL LIFE

A. MIND MANIFESTS ITSELF

"Mind manifests itself" was one of the more important sayings of Dr. Gesell. What he meant by this was that virtually anything the child does expresses his mind in action. It doesn't have to be merely things he says. It can be anything he does—crawling, creeping, grasping at objects, smiling, eating, crying.

In this respect, Dr. Gesell's approach seems to have differed from that of the Swiss psychologist Jean Piaget, who talked a great deal about so-called cognition, or thinking. This he measured by checking things the child expressed verbally. Dr. Gesell made no such distinction.

We have assumed that the baby's mind is at work almost from the moment he or she was born, long before spoken language develops. So what can we tell you about the mind of the One-year-old?

The first birthday, which, of course, occurs when the baby is just Twelve months of age, tends to be a very important occasion in the average family—a time of great rejoicing. We hope outsiders will not be invited since too many people can confuse the young infant. But the family as a rule does celebrate with a cake and candle and whatever other festivities it deems suitable.

However, behavior-wise, the time of the first birthday is not a particularly significant turning point. Just earlier, around Forty to Forty-four weeks, several significant new behaviors come in. Many infants begin to creep, begin to grasp small objects between thumb and forefinger. At Forty-eight weeks the baby may begin to cruise alongside his playpen rail. A little later, by Fifty-six weeks, many can say three or four words; by Fifteen months most can build a tower of two little blocks.

But right at the time of the first birthday there are few new or exciting behavior items which appear. As Table 1 shows, the One-year-old infant may try placing one block on top of another, but usually without success. He may try inserting a tiny pellet into a small glass bottle, but again without success. If he walks, it is usually with one hand held—true independent walking has not yet come in for most. His vocabulary as a rule consists of no more than two "words" besides "Mama" and "Dada."

We know his mind is at work as he creeps and cuddles, smiles and laughs, coos and cries. But the time of the first birthday is not an age of marked new intellectual achievement.

B. INTELLIGENCE AND MATURITY LEVEL

Though by the time your child begins primary school, certainly by the time he begins elementary school, it will be useful for you to know his approximate intellectual level (is he very bright, bright, average, below average?), it is not necessary that you know this level when he is in his second year of life. (An exception could be if you were adopting. In that case it is extremely important to know all you can about a child in order that you make your adoption decision wisely and plan accordingly.)

If it is your own boy or girl, however, though you will probably have a notion about his or her level of intelligence (he will in all likelihood seem to you unusually bright), you do not need to know his IQ.

Something that could be useful for you to know, how-ever, even at this early age, is his or her maturity level. For instance, if your Eighteen-month-old is already behaving like a typical Twenty-one-month-old, you will be fair in expecting a little more than one does of the typical child of Eighteen months. On the other hand, if behavior at Eighteen months is most like that of a typical Fifteen-month-old, you will be wise to expect a little less than typical Eighteen months' behavior.

Recognition of immature behavior (if such it be) is espe-cially important a few years later when the child is about to begin kindergarten. When a child is Five years of age and thus legally old enough to start school, if he is behav-ing like a Four or Four-and-a-half-year-old, you will be wise at least to consider the possibility of delaying the time of kindergarten entrance.

All this is rather far in the future. However, especially in the case of normally intelligent but slow-developing boys, it is indeed important to be aware of that slowness of development so that you can be quite sure *not* to expect too much and not to be disappointed in your child's behavior.

Various child specialists have developed batteries of tests by means of which they can determine the behavior age of any child from infancy through Ten years of age. Since our own Gesell battery is one of the better known, we'll tell you about this rather than one of the others.

Parents do not as a rule have access to such special test materials as form board or pellet and bottle. Nor should they try to "examine" their own children. However, many of our test items are easy even for the nonpsychologist to check for. Thus it may be of interest to readers to refer to Tables 1 and 2 on pages 85 and 86.

These tables list some of the more usual abilities that may be expected to appear at Forty-eight weeks, Fifty-two weeks, and Fifty-six weeks and at Fifteen months, Eigh-teen months, and Twenty-one months of age. Reference to these tables will give you a general idea as to whether your own child's behavior falls more or less in the usual range.

Behavior, of course, may fall a little below or a little above this range. Keep in mind that boys on the average develop a little more slowly than do girls. Also, a child may be advanced in one or more of the four areas of behavior —Motor, Adaptive, Language, Personal-Social—and less advanced in another. Behavior does not always develop all of a piece.

It is very important for parents to keep in mind that a child's behavior age is not necessarily the same as his intellectual level. A child could be adequately intelligent and still be immature (young) for his age. Intelligence tests for the very young should be given only by the child specialist, and even then some think they are not entirely reliable.

Suffice it to say that if your child can perform most of the

tasks listed in Tables 1 and 2, it is a very good bet that he or she is of normal intelligence. However, if he does not, there is still a good likelihood that intelligence as such is normal but that the child is merely a little young for his age. *Immaturity is not the same thing as low intelligence.*

Only if your own instinct warns you that your child does not walk, talk, handle objects, or understand what you say as well as it seems to you others of his age can do should you be concerned. In that case your own pediatrician can help you find somebody qualified to advise you.

C. INTELLECTUAL ABILITIES

Sense of Time TWELVE TO FIFTEEN MONTHS: Even by One year of age, if not well before, babies indicate that they have a mild sense of time. They seem to be aware that certain events follow certain other events. When the baby is hungry, sight of his mother often causes him to open his mouth and nuzzle for food. When he wants to be picked up, arms held out to him cause him to make certain bodily adjustments to aid the pickup. When at the Twelve to Fifteen months' casting stage he throws an object to the floor, he watches and waits for somebody to pick up the object and return it to him; he may vocalize and gesture vigorously if the pickup is delayed.

So certain people or situations do seem to cause him to anticipate that certain things will follow. He or she is almost certainly aware that crying tends to bring results of one sort of another. How much actual time sense is involved, one cannot be certain, though we do know that if crying is not rewarded, very often, as time goes on, it becomes louder and more demanding.

EIGHTEEN MONTHS: The time sense of the Eighteen-month-old can pretty much be encompassed in a single word: "now." He wants what he wants *now.* "Later," "in a minute," "pretty soon"—all words or phrases which will work wonders in a few months—are meaningless to him; "tomorrow" and "yesterday" are so much Greek.

Table 1
GESELL DEVELOPMENTAL SCHEDULES

Forty-eight Weeks	Fifty-two Weeks	Fifty-six Weeks
	MOTOR	
Blocks: sequential play	Blocks: tries tower of two; fails	Cup-cube: one cube into cup without demonstration
Pellet and bottle: touches pellet only	Cup-cube: releases one cube into cup	Drawing: vigorous imitative scribbling
Form board: removes round block from round hole	Ring-string: dangles ring by string	Form board (dem): inserts round block into round hole
Pellet: neat pincer grasp between thumb and forefinger	Form board: looks selectively at round hole	Blocks: grasps two in one hand
Sits: pivots	Walks: needs only one hand held	Stands: momentarily alone
Stands: cruises at rail		
Walks: needs two hands held		
	LANGUAGE	
Vocabulary: says "Mama" and "Dada"	Vocabulary: two "words" besides "Mama" and "Dada"	Vocabulary: three or four words
		Incipient jargon
		Knows a few objects by name
	PERSONAL-SOCIAL	
Play: toys to side rail	Mirror: offers ball to mirror image	Releases ball with slight cast toward adult
	Cooperates in dressing	

Table 2
GESELL DEVELOPMENTAL SCHEDULES

Fifteen Months	*Eighteen Months*	*Twenty-one Months*
	MOTOR	
Walks: few steps, starts, stops	Walks: seldom falls	Walks: squats in play
Walks: falls by collapse	Walks: fast, runs stiffly	Stairs: walks down, one hand held
Walks: creeping discarded	Stairs: walks up, one hand held	Stairs: walks up, holds rail
Stairs: creeps up and down	Small chair: seats self	Large ball (dem): kicks
Blocks: tower of two	Adult chair: climbs into	Blocks: tower of five to six
Book: helps turn pages	Ball: hurls	
	Large ball: walks into	
	Book: turns pages, two to three at once	
	ADAPTIVE	
Blocks: tower of two	Blocks: tower of three to four	Blocks: tower of five to six
Cup-cube: six in and out of cup	Cup-cube: ten into cup	Blocks: imitates pushing "train"
Drawing: beginning imitation stroke	Drawing: scribbles spontaneously	Paper: folds imitatively
Form board (no dem): places round block in round hole	Drawing: makes stroke imitatively	Form board: places two to three in appropriate holes
	Form board: piles round, square, triangular blocks	

Vocabulary: four to six words, including names
Vocabulary: uses jargon
Book: pats pictures

Feeding: bottle discarded
Feeding: inhibits grasp of dish
Communication: says "Mama," "Dada," a few other words
Communication: indicates wants (points or vocalizes)
Play: shows or offers toy
Play: casts object in play or in refusal

LANGUAGE

Book: looks selectively
Vocabulary: ten words, including names
Ball: names ball
Ball: obeys two directions

PERSONAL-SOCIAL

Feeding: hands empty dish
Feeding: feeds self in part, spills
Toilet: bowel control
Play: pulls a toy
Play: carries or hugs doll or stuffed animal

Vocabulary: twenty words or so
Speech: combines two to three words spontaneously
Ball: obeys three directions

Feeding: handles cup well
Communication: asks for food, toilet, drink
Communication: echoes two or more last words
Communication: pulls person to show
Toilet: may be aware of puddles made

But, as earlier, a sense of sequence is definitely present. For instance, the sight of juice and crackers or other food may bring him to the table without his being asked. (Or at least it may cause him to move in the direction of his high chair.)

TWENTY-ONE MONTHS: The child of this age still lives chiefly in the present. His or her main time word continues to be "now." Projection into the future, however, is beginning to develop. He may wait in response to "in a minute." There is also an improving sense of timing. Two children may rock in rhythm, or a child may sit at the table (in nursery school or day care center) and wait for the juice which he can see being prepared for him.

Sense of sequence is improving slightly. A child on seeing his father with a bath towel in hand may say, "Daddy go bah," or, on seeing either parent with a coat on, may say, "Go wok." Or a very verbal little girl may say, "Man [mailman] come soon. Doan [Joan] arbers non y go wok."

Time sense is definitely expanding.

Sense of Space NINE TO FIFTEEN MONTHS: Our knowledge about the young infant's sense of space is rather limited. Dr. Gesell has commented:

> Appreciations of space are at first discontinuous. Baby senses merely the immediate space in which he is immersed. He does not sense its context; is unaware of distance and depth. For him the visible world is probably like a flat screen. Not till he is about nine months old does he begin to probe into the beyond and the beneath. Slowly the relation of container and contained dawns on him.
>
> At that time he begins to thrust his fist intentfully into an empty cup and about that time he seems to discover the third dimension. Space loses its flatness; it takes on the perspectives of depth, hollow, solid. Through ceaseless manipulation of objects he penetrates and investigates the properties of space.

By One year of age he or she will try (though unsuccessfully) to put one small block on top of another; can put a small block into a cup; will even try to put a tiny candy pellet into a bottle.

By Fifteen months most can build a tower of two blocks, put several small blocks into a cup, place a round block in a round hole in a wooden board.

EIGHTEEN MONTHS: Time is *now* and space is *here.* The sense of space seems to be more basic and even more meaningful than the sense of time. Even when younger, the child could gesture for "up," hold out his arms to be taken out of his crib.

Now both "up" and "down" are strongly within his vocabulary, as are "oben" and "cose" and also that very helpful word "gone." "Where" is responded to and may even be used by the somewhat advanced as part of a hide-and-seek game such as "Where's Billy?" Or a child may pull a sheet or blanket over her mother's face, saying, "Where's Mama?" and then, as she removes it, "Here Mama."

Our own summary of space words and concepts available to the Eighteen-month-olds in our nursery school at Yale was as follows: The child spontaneously used "up," "down," and "off," dealing with his or her own basic movements in space. "Come," "go," and "gone" also referred to his or her own activities or to the presence or absence of objects in which he or she was directly interested.

No space words are commonly used in response to direct questions. The child may merely look in the direction indicated. He can, in examination, obey two directions with a ball, putting it on a chair and giving it to his mother.

TWENTY-ONE MONTHS: Even three months bring change in a fast-moving field—the acquisition of space words and concepts. A summary of the space notions of the typical Twenty-one-month-old shows that although there are still no space words in response to questions, "up," "down," "on," and "off" all are used spontaneously, as is the size word "big." Also, most characteristic of this age are "all gone," expressing interest in absence or departure of person or object, and "here," suggesting the "here and now-ness" of this age. Children also frequently look in a direction indicated.

One individual and rather highly verbal Twenty-one-month-old girl included the following space words and phrases in her vocabulary: "Kuddlup [get up]," "Down, kitty," "Zum [thumb] in nere peese," "Shipper noff. Shoo y tokee non."

By Twenty-two months this same girl's vocabulary included the following: "Were Doan pencoo? Fin Doan pencoo," "Kitty, go outdoors," "Were kitty? Kitty on couch," "Down, kitty," "Oben dowah," "Ha [hat] non, besh [dress] non," "Door ko ti," "Uppa kool [up at school]," "Come in."

A fairly advanced Twenty-one-month-old may be able to take part in an adult-initiated game of hide-and-seek, between the child and her friend. It is hard for her to keep her eyes closed till the other child has hidden. Then she will go cautiously to the exact place where the friend was found before. If this fails, she listens for a while till she hears a rustle and then goes to that place.

Asked where her daddy is, she may reply (correctly), "Uppa cool." Or, if a dog outdoors and out of sight barks, this child might order, "Top, dog." Silence. Then she will say, "Dog go way."

Looking for her own special book in a bookcase, she might say, "Were Doanie book? Fin Doanie book." There is definitely beginning to be a desire for a special place for the child's own things.

Sense of Self TWELVE MONTHS: Our real knowledge of what a One-year-old baby thinks about himself is limited indeed. However, we can tell you some of the things he likes to do, things which make up his small world of living. The child of this age loves gross motor activity. He likes to creep, walk, pull himself to standing, cruise along the side of his playpen. Even though he may possibly be able to walk, he prefers creeping and loves to creep after his sometimes elusive ball.

He enjoys his toys and likes to put things in and out of other, larger things. He enjoys other people and likes to show off his social tricks, as pat-a-caking, waving bye-bye, or responding to the game of "Where's the baby?"

His response to the mirror suggests a growing sense of self as he regards his mirrored image, pats that image, even leans forward and kisses his reflected face. He seems now to see his whole reflection, not merely some part of himself as his hand or foot. He seems to be well aware that when he moves his own hand, the hand in the mirror moves as well.

FIFTEEN MONTHS: The child of this age is often less shy and much more secure in his or her sense of self than just three months earlier. He is interested in all around him. On a walk, for instance, he loves to pick up sticks, leaves,

or sometimes less suitable objects which he spies on the ground. He likes to imitate other people—everything seems grist for his mill. In the house, too, he loves to toddle and touch, being especially interested in the contents of ashtrays and wastebaskets.

Placed before a mirror, he may be less sociable than just earlier, more concerned in strong and prolonged regard for his own face. He likes to touch his own mirrored face, and though the face gets prime attention, his regard tends to travel from head down to feet, as if he were trying to put the whole body together. He likes to regard fingertips as he moves them on the mirror.

EIGHTEEN MONTHS: The Eighteen-month-old gives the impression, through his (many) actions and his (relatively few) words of being extremely egocentric. The majority of his reactions are to himself and his own activities. Much of the time he ignores other people, even though at times he can show affection, especially to his mother.

Social reactions to other adults do occur, but they are for the most part not self-initiated. And the child of this age largely ignores other children except as objects to be explored.

The Eighteen-month-old defends and strengthens his or her sense of self by opposing others. "No" is the favorite word, and most activity is motor. However, even a self-centered Eighteen-month-old can at times be lovingly and laughingly sociable, especially if he or she is of a basically good-natured temperament.

And a certain aspect of the sense of self is demonstrated by the child's beginning understanding that certain things belong definitely to him and not to others. Some even show a beginning comprehension that these belongings of their own belong in some special place.

TWENTY-ONE MONTHS: The Eighteen-month-old sometimes seems to define himself with the word "no." That is, self is defined by negating what others request or require. By Twenty-one months self is beginning to be defined by insisting on possessions—"mine." By Two years of age, self may be defined by calling attention to possessions—"Lookit my new shoes"—or by calling attention to abilities—"Watch me."

Some Eighteen-month-olds are able, if told that their ears, noses, eyes *are* their ears, noses, eyes, can then, when asked, point to these parts of their own and other people's bodies.

And, as mentioned elsewhere, many at this age may be quite possessive about their own book, doll, teddy, or whatever. They also may have a very good idea about the possessions of other people—that a certain book, chair, pair of slippers belongs to Daddy, Mommy, or some other member of the family. All this implies a certain concept of self since to them quite clearly the things that belong to them *are* a part of their very selves.

Sense of Humor TWELVE TO FIFTEEN MONTHS: Little has been written about the humor of the child of this age because actually very little has ever been observed. The Twelve- to Fifteen-month old girl or boy, if happy and healthy, will laugh and smile a lot, will much of the time exhibit robust good humor. Many laugh if adults push them over in play. Or they may laugh loudly when approached, in fun, by a growling adult. In fact, frequently roughhousing play does bring smiles and laughter.

But so far as what might be called a sense of humor goes, most probably are not very far developed. Smiles and chuckles are one thing, but a true sense of the humorous or ridiculous probably is something else again and in most comes later.

EIGHTEEN MONTHS: The self-involved Eighteen-month-old smiles most at his or her own activity. And the type of own activity which amuses most is his or her own gross motor activity.

Typical of the things which he finds the most amusing are: falling down on purpose, sliding down or bouncing down a small slide, rocking on a rocking boat, pushing furniture or toys, or pounding on things with his rubber hammer.

The second most smile-provoking stimulus is his or her own approaches to an adult when he or she is in a good mood. So a child may hold out a doll or other toy to the adult, show a pet turtle, stuff his mouth too full of food, and smile at the grown-up to show that this is a humorous action.

Or a little girl about to suck her thumb, if she catches your eye, may continue her hand up from her mouth to her head and pat her hair.

Eighteen-month-olds checked by us in random nursery school play were seen to smile only once every six minutes, and laughter was even less frequent. Eighteen months tends to be, except in the most smiling, a rather sober age.

TWENTY-ONE MONTHS: In these short three months humor has changed conspicuously. Now the child's own

motor behavior may come second as a smile producer to social approaches to nursery school teacher or mother. Motor activity still is a source of great amusement, especially when it is vigorous, as a vigorous pushing of some object, rocking high, or riding a truck or wagon very fast.

But for sheer number of smiles, the child's own approach of almost any sort to the adult is the leading source of pleasure and amusement. Our clocking of nursery school play suggested that on the average the Twenty-one-month-old smiled about once every four minutes.

Among the many different situations which we have observed as humor-provoking with Twenty-one-month-olds are, social actions with teacher, such as smiling at teacher in a friendly way, pointing out objects in book, showing toys; joking (as coughing in pretend need); pretend play as pretending to take a bite of something, hiding and pretending he is not there when someone finds him, pretending to make a call on a toy telephone, pretending to pour milk out of an imaginary pitcher, pretending to drink milk out of a toy cup; incongruity as fitting himself into a bookshelf or creeping like a turtle.

D. CAN YOU INCREASE YOUR CHILD'S INTELLIGENCE?

It is a normal drive to try to teach one's young. And if you keep it within bounds, there is nothing wrong with it.

Such books as *How to Give Your Child a Superior Mind, How to Raise Your Child's IQ, How to Teach Your Baby to Read, How to Teach Your Baby Math* are, of course, not realistic or useful. One can help any child make good use of such intelligence as he or she may have inherited; one can read to the very young child; one can see that he or she is brought up in an intellectually and socially stimulating atmosphere.

But it would be quite impossible to teach a baby to read. And a child's basic intellectual level is not as a rule increased by anything that you as parents do to or for your child.

Supplementing such books as those rather ludicrous ones mentioned above are many others which tell young parents how to play pat-a-cake with their baby, how to roll a ball to a baby, how to play peekaboo, how to talk to the baby. If your own natural intelligence and instinct do not tell you how to do all these things, by all means read a book and find out how. The paradox here is that such parents as may actually need such basic instruction are for the most part not reading books. The parents who do read this kind of book are usually already doing the things described and so do not need to be taught.

However, though ideally you should not be self-conscious about teaching the very young, it is unquestionably true that the intellectual and social stimulation which you provide right from the beginning is most important. It *is* important to spend time with your infant and preschooler. It *is* important to talk with him, play with him, read to him, show him that you love him.

Just as the Eighteen-month-old is "into" everything physically, so his or her mind is "into" everything intellectually. The child of this age is a tireless explorer, investigating everything that comes his way.

Dr. Fitzhugh Dodson recommends, and we strongly agree, that one of the most important things you can do to help your child use his mind and one of the most important ways in which you can encourage a love of reading later on, is to read to him early. The time from Fifteen to Eighteen months is by no means too soon to start.

At this age the child himself may be able to do no more than, when asked, point out the "doggie," "kitty," "Mommy," "baby" in pictures that he sees. But just by listening to you as you read to him, he can acquire a good feeling about books. And though some are ready to listen sooner than others, at least try reading to your boy or girl. If he or she shows little interest, try again in another month or two.

A list of books which we recommend is given in Appendix B.

And though your child's intellectual development is surely not all up to you, here are other things, besides reading to him, which you can do for your child of this age:

First and foremost do any and all of the things which come so naturally. Talk to him; laugh with him; repeat after him the things he says to you.

Provide the kinds of toys so loved by any Fifteen- to Eighteen-month-old, and let him play alone. He likes it if you are in sight, but you don't have to take an active part in all his play activities.

Find out what he likes to do best and make this possible. It may amount to no more than giving him a "bang bang" and letting him bang away. It may be providing almost any object on wheels and letting him push it and pull it.

Encourage him to show you things, and then talk with him about what he shows you.

Buy, if you like, certain educational toys, such as a color cone which features graduated wooden rings on a peg. But don't push any of these materials which supposedly sharpen up the child's mind. Let him set the pace for any intellectual improvement.

Provide as many opportunities as possible for sheer physical activity—a doorway swing, stairs to climb, large objects to push, big blocks to build with.

Take him for many a carriage ride, pointing out to him the interesting things along the way, such as dogs and babies, airplanes and mud puddles.

And last of all, though some will shudder at the thought, a little television now and then provides variety and excitement and introduces the young viewer to sights and sounds which might not otherwise be available.

Helping your boy or girl learn about the world around him or her is easy and fun, but it should not be carried out in the spirit of formal teaching and should not be considered primarily as "cognitive enrichment." It is merely part of living.

chapter nine
INDIVIDUALITY

Perhaps the most important thing we could say to you about your One- to Two-year-old, or, for that matter, about your child of any age, is that you must remember every human person is an individual. Nobody is exactly like anybody else, even his or her identical twin.

So your child in the second year of life may be more advanced or less advanced than the supposedly "typical" child we tell you about in this book. He may be happier or less happy. He may be more temperamental or less. He may be more sociable, amenable, and loving, or less so.

The important things are two: (1) that you try to understand him as he is and (2) that you do not congratulate or blame yourselves for the way your boy or girl turns out.

It has often been said that it is possible, if you do all the "right" things, to help your child live at his top level, expressing his very highest and best potentials. But if these potentials are less than terrific, this will not be because of something you have done or failed to do. Human intelligence and potential vary, genetically, from brilliant to rather dull. You do not determine this level by things you do or do not do.

Human personality ranges from the charming, delightful, and clever to the less than charming, less than delightful, less than clever. Some children are secure, happy, giving, almost from the moment of birth. Others find life difficult, also from the moment of birth (or before).

The most that we as parents can do about all this is to understand, and respect, our children's potential range in any, or every, respect and then try to help them live up to their top potential.

It is not entirely to your credit if your child is witty, happy and wise. Nor is it to your discredit if he or she is quite otherwise. You can and probably will do the best you can with the material you have to work with, but what that material will be is determined more by nature than by nurture.

There are many ways of classifying personality. Scientists have been working at this problem for many years. Our own favorite classificatory system is that of William Sheldon (3). According to Dr. Sheldon, we behave as we do largely because of the way our bodies are built. That is, behavior is a function of structure.

According to his system of classification, which is known as Constitutional Psychology, there are three chief physical types, though no one individual represents one type exclusively—we all are combinations of all three. In most people one or the other dominates and thus largely determines our behavior.

As we have described elsewhere (3), Sheldon's system of constitutional psychology proposes that we can to quite an extent predict how any child will behave from an observation of what his body is like. The three components which go to make up human constitution are endomorphy, mesomorphy, and ectomorphy. The body of the endomorph is round and soft; that of the mesomorph, hard and square; that of the ectomorph, linear, fragile, and delicate.

In the *endomorph* the arms and legs are relatively short compared with the trunk, with the upper part of the arm longer than the lower part. Hands and feet are small and plump. Fingers are short and tapering. In the *mesomorph* the extremities are large and massive, with the upper arm and leg equal to the lower arm and leg in length. Hands and wrists are large; fingers, squarish. In the *ectomorph,* the arms and legs are long compared with the body, the lower arm longer than the upper arm. Hands and feet are slender and fragile, with pointed fingertips.

Recognizing your own child's body type and knowing how endomorphs, mesomorphs, or ectomorphs customarily behave may help you fit your own expectations closer to reality than might otherwise be the case.

According to Sheldon, the endomorphic individual is one who attends and exercises *in order to eat.* Eating is his chief pleasure. The mesomorph attends and eats *in order to exercise.* What he likes best is athletic activity and competitive action. The ectomorph, on the other hand, exercises (as little as possible) and eats (with indifference) *in order to attend.* Watching, listening, thinking about things, and being aware are his most enjoyable activities.

Another clue to the differences among these three types is that when in trouble, the endomorph seeks people, the mesomorph seeks activity, the ectomorph seeks solitude.

At Eighteen months the differences among these kinds of children may be seen in that the endomorph in general is easygoing and easy to get on with. The mesomorph is loud and active and may be the one most given to noisy temper tantrums. The ectomorph may be the one who has the hardest time with himself, may seem especially vulnerable to foods which do not agree with him, may have a hard time sleeping through the night.

Admittedly it is a little difficult to distinguish these three basic kinds of body structure (and thus of personality) as early as Eighteen months of age. However, even at Eighteen months it can be helpful to parents to keep in mind that there may be these three basic types and that they all are obviously different no matter what you do. The plump, good-natured endomorph will enjoy good food, will enjoy other people, couldn't care less whether he comes out ahead. The muscular, loud, noisy, athletic, aggressive mesomorph tends to be constantly active and, as he or she grows older, seems to live for competition. The thin, shy, sensitive, aware ectomorph cares relatively little for people, less for food, and little at all for sports and physical activity. Each can be splendid in his or her own way. But one cannot be turned into the other no matter what your preference.

Some object to Sheldon's theory of personality because they consider it "fatalistic" and interpret it as meaning that there is little a parent can do to help a child function effectively. Quite the contrary. The more one understands basic, inherent personality, the more effectively one can determine what he can and cannot expect to accomplish.

So, if a parent wants to, he can often help a quiet, calm, perhaps somewhat lazy endomorph be a little more active and aggressive. He or she can at least try to quiet down an overactive and noisy mesomorph or help a shy, retiring ectomorph to come out of his shell. But understanding the child's inherent potential, a parent will appreciate that there are limits to what can be done.

The same thing holds if we apply another, and newer, kind of classification, that of Dr. Lendon H. Smith. Dr. Smith in his popular *Feed Your Kids Right* classifies individuals with respect to their basic level of health (30), as being in one of five different categories, as follows:

Level One: This infant grows to adulthood free of illness, rashes, gas, headaches, fatigue, depression, insomnia. He came from a stress-free, comfortable, full-term pregnancy and easy delivery. He laughs and smiles more than he cries and frowns. He does not bruise easily.

He cuts teeth easily. He handles weather changes, teething, learning new skills and other stresses with a minimum of psychosomatic symptoms. He can eat many foods and occasionally even junk food or sugar without a headache or fainting or fatigue. His permanent teeth are even, free of cavities, uncrowded, and there is room for his wisdom teeth.

He makes friends easily and has a pleasant personality. He is adroit and coordinated. He is neither thin nor

fat. He has few extremes of emotional response—he cries or laughs appropriately. He enjoys doing things for others.

He sails through his developmental levels in physical, psychological and cognitive growth as if he had read the charts. He is easy to toilet train. He enjoys pleasing his loved ones. He can also entertain himself.

Level Two: There is nothing very wrong here, but the differences suggest a slight [possibility of] slippage. . . . He laughs more than he cries and in general is a satisfactory baby and child. But he has occasional moments of allergy, discontent, moodiness, sickness. He doesn't sleep through the night until three months of age. A cold develops only if someone brings it home—maybe two or three times a year—and clears rapidly with nose drops and antihistamines without accompanying ear infection. May sneeze for a week during pollen season.

Teething may be accompanied by a fever, but aspirin is curative; no disease follows. He has food preferences but can be talked into eating almost everything except liver and spinach. Rashes appear with some new foods but disappear in a day or so.

Temper tantrums are short. Growth is even. He has little trouble in getting toilet trained. Only one attack of croup per winter and only one strep throat in every two or three years. He learns easily. Only a few accidents. Is careful with toys.

Enjoys sweets but has no obvious food cravings. Accepts punishment if fair. Goes to bed with only a little reluctance. Plays cooperatively with others. Likes to win but accepts a loss cheerfully.

Level Three: The mother of the child in this category often had a stressful pregnancy: nausea and vomiting. Baby may have trouble in getting started to nurse. May pick up on weight and strength, and things go well for about two to four weeks, when colic, eczema, wheezing or vomiting, gas and diarrhea push a barely Level I baby into Level II or III. These are the babies who get colic medicine, antihistamines, antibiotics, ointments and milk changes and whose families need tranquilizers, sedatives and aspirin.

These children are touchy, often uncuddlable—as if the world is too close. If the parents can hold such a child together, he may outgrow his problems, but each new stress will overburden his weak defenses.

He overreacts to separation; has violent temper tantrums over the slightest insult; is noncompliant in eating, toilet training. Has persistent allergies. His nights do not seem restful. He may resist going to bed. He awakens screaming with a night terror perhaps once a month. He is a picky eater; gets head- and stomachaches easily. Is sallow and has dark circles under his eyes.

Level Four: Individuals unfortunate enough to qualify for this category [may] require almost constant medical attention: daily drug therapy for epilepsy, diabetes, cystic fibrosis; gamma globulin and antibiotics to ward off infections; weekly allergy shots, etc.

For many children the body may have arrived at this level but the emotional and intellectual level may still be up at the I and II area. Some have bodies and general physical health that qualify them for Level I or II but their psyche is at the fourth level: depression, phobias, extreme hyperactivity, belligerence, migraine.

Level Five: This category contains the bedridden, terminally ill, extremely retarded or malformed—the child about whom doctors become very depressed. We would like to help, but the conditions seem irreversible.

Lest all this seem rather hopeless, we hasten to add Dr. Smith's comment that many children in Level II or III need only diet changes to move them into gratifyingly good health. Others in Levels IV and V would more likely need high-potency vitamins, even injections in high doses to reverse slippage.

He suggests:

> If one can banish anti-nutrients and get the whole family on a program of sound nutrition, within three or four weeks everybody should feel better and be more cheerful. Persistent rashes and watery noses should clear up. Head- and stomach-aches should be gone or be only mild. Tempers will not flare so easily. But it is important that the whole family follow good eating habits. (For books that will help you feed your family right, see references listed in Appendix C, pp. 166–167.)

One special aspect of individuality which it may be useful for parents to keep in mind is this: Though children in general, as they mature, swing from periods of equilibrium (or good behavior) to periods of disequilibrium (or difficult behavior), as illustrated in Figure 1, we cannot guarantee where any given child's midline of behavior may be. Say it is to the right of the presumed typical midline illustrated; then the child's behavior will be skewed toward the "good" or equilibrium side of life. Even at his or her worst, things will tend to be not too bad.

On the other hand, say that your child's theoretical midline of behavior is to the left of that which is customary; then his or her behavior will be skewed toward the difficult or disequilibrium side of life. Even at his or her best, behavior may be somewhat tangled or troubled. If this is the case, you will need to make even more effort than usual to keep your child on an even keel.

One final, and highly important, personality factor which very strongly influences behavior is the matter of sex. For all that some people nowadays insist that boys behave differently from girls chiefly because we expect them to, there is much substantial evidence that sex differences in behavior are major, inherited, and persistent.

True, society as a whole may expect boys to be "boyish" and girls to be "girlish," and these expectations do to some extent influence behavior. However, those with experience in the scientific observation and testing of young children are fully aware that in general and with certain exceptions, girls develop more rapidly than do boys and are therefore more advanced in measurable kinds of behavior.

It is not realistic to assume that parental expectation alone could be enough to cause girls to walk earlier than boys, talk earlier, be toilet trained earlier. Nor is it realistic to assume that parental expectation (when the child is a bit older) causes girls to copy a circle, square, or triangle earlier than boys do; to add more parts to our Gesell Incomplete Man Test form; to repeat digits sooner; to count sooner; to print letters, numbers, and names sooner (4).

Most parents presumably may not even be aware that girls do most of these things earlier than do boys. Parents may indeed pressure their girls to be docile and gentle, their boys to be strong and bold. But it is not reasonable to assume that they try to or can cause their daughters to respond to behavior tests in a more mature manner than their sons.

It is our opinion, then, that the earlier maturation of girls compared to boys is one of the chief causes of the marked differences of behavior in the two sexes which we customarily observe. So, if your Eighteen-month-old boy is not saying much more than "Mommy," "Daddy," "doggie," "baby," "coat," "hat," "out," and the Eighteen-month-old girl next door is talking up a storm, don't be discouraged about your son. Girls in general talk sooner than boys do.

And girls in general tend to be gentler than boys. A truism that is actually true (with, of course, notable exceptions) is that girls are easier to bring up than boys.

Some mothers report that, especially at Eighteen months, their girls are much easier to get on with than their boys. It may be that their often advanced talking makes them better able to tell you what it is they want.

Or it may be that girls, with their often more sociable dispositions, relate more easily to other people even at this early age. They may not withdraw in isolated splendor as much as boys do.

And often less muscular than boys, they seem to put less vigor into their tantrums when things go wrong.

So then, the picture of extreme Eighteen-monthishness which we paint may apply a little more aptly to your sons than to your daughters.

There is one further aspect of individuality that we would like to stress. This is a notion suggested by Boston pediatrician T. Berry Brazelton (8) that not only is each child an individual, but also each mother-child combination has its own individuality.

As Brazelton points out, each mother-child couple (in

fact, probably each father-child couple) has its own individuality. Some mothers are fortunate enough to have produced a baby whom they understand and who understands them. Things go well between them quite naturally.

There are other mother-child couples who seem, somehow, out of sync. The mother just doesn't feel quite confident and secure with the child; the child does not feel quite comfortable and secure with the mother.

It is very important for a mother who is not comfortable and secure with one of her children not to consider herself a bad mother just because things do not always go well between her and her baby.

This is an especially important notion for the mother of an Eighteen-month-old to keep in mind. No matter how well adjusted the child, no matter how good the relationship, this is an age level when things tend to be difficult.

It is extremely important especially for a mother who may not "fit" perfectly with her child not to add to the complexity of this often difficult age by blaming herself when things go badly. Even under ideal conditions the age level of Eighteen months, even though it has its own certain fascination, can be a difficult time for all concerned.

However, in spite of the usefulness of knowing that all children are different and that each can be classified according to some system, such as those proposed by Sheldon and Smith, or can certainly be classed as male or female, or that some children are more difficult than others we must not allow this kind of knowledge to interfere with our appreciation of each child as a unique individual.

Herbert Kohl (22) points out correctly:

It is important to learn how to look at children without necessarily ranking or comparing them. Instead of wondering about who is best or most beautiful, it makes sense to look for the uniqueness in each individual. This requires practice—some children emerge slowly, some give a first impression that quickly changes, others are admirably constant.

Some children are easy to find attractive. There are others who seem too sloppy or nervous or extreme in one feature or another to be attractive. It is hard for many adults to look at or be with children who don't show an easy charm or grace or who don't conform to their stereotypes.

Yet all children who are not deprived of love show a grace and uniqueness. It is a question of adults' learning to look into children's eyes, to encounter them face-to-face, to show respect and love, and therefore to allow mutual respect and regard to emerge.

In other words, regardless of any child's basic endowment, there is much that you as a parent can do to bring out his very best qualities, to show him that he is loved and cared about.

chapter ten
STORIES FROM REAL LIFE

FIFTEEN MONTHS

FIFTEEN-MONTH-OLD APPEARS UNINTERESTED IN FOOD

Dear Doctors:

I need advice about a feeding problem with my Fifteen-month old son, Eric. Eric is a happy, healthy child who has never had too much interest in food. Unless given a toy to play with, he will not sit in his high chair to eat. Perhaps because of this, he has not shown any interest in feeding himself. I have tried to encourage him by giving him a spoon to play with instead of a toy, but he only bangs with it, tosses it aside, and refuses to eat unless distracted with a plaything.

Also, he is still on canned junior foods and refuses to eat anything else. His great love is milk. (Is this the root of my problem?) He likes to drink it from a glass that he holds well. Also, he has about four ounces with his nap in a bottle. At night about seven o'clock he goes to bed with an eight-ounce bottle—about 10:00 he has another bottle and sometimes another at 3:00 A.M.

From what you say it does not seem to us that you have too much of a feeding problem. It is quite normal for a boy of his age to be more interested in playing with his toys than in feeding himself. As long as he allows you to feed him, as he apparently does, you don't have too much to worry about.

However, it is really late for him to have a three o'clock bottle. You should try to get him to give this up. In fact, try to cut down on all his bottles. As you yourself suspect, if he did give up his bottle entirely, he would undoubtedly show more enthusiasm for other foods.

DEMANDING FIFTEEN-MONTH-OLD KEEPS MOTHER AWAKE
EVERY NIGHT

Dear Doctors:

We are having a problem with our Fifteen-month-old daughter, Diane, that is affecting our entire family. For the past several months she has been waking at least once a night, sometimes as many as four times. When she wakes, she cries and screams, and nothing will stop her but water. We've tried letting her cry, but she keeps it up for at least an hour, and it just gets to be too much.

Her sister, Laura, aged Three, sleeps in the same room but never wakes. As a result of the broken sleep, I have been losing weight and waking up each morning as tired as when I went to bed. This is having a terrible effect as I am irritable, listless, and scolding the children for the least offense. Laura has always been a docile, obedient girl, and I find that my constant nagging hurts her feelings terribly.

Diane never leaves her older sister alone, and Laura gives her everything without a fight. If she goes near Diane, she gets hit, has toys thrown at her, her hair pulled, etc. Lately I've caught her sneaking up behind Diane and pushing her down and sitting on her. I don't blame her, but I have to punish her before they begin to seriously hurt each other.

My nerves are at the breaking point. My sweet Laura is becoming sullen and whiny. And yet I feel guilty because I favor Diane because she has spunk. How can I calm her down so we'll all relax?

A large part of your problem, as you realize, is that your two children are so close together. They would benefit from separate caretakers. Obviously they are having a very bad effect on each other.

Wakefulness at night is all too common around Fifteen months of age. And you're lucky that water will put Diane back to sleep. Some children can handle night wakefulness by themselves, but all too many need a personal response from one of their parents. Some won't quiet down at all.

Our tendency would be for you *or your husband* to go to Diane at once when she wakes and give her water right away. Even stay with her a little while—let her play with water in the bathroom basin. With most, the quicker you stop the crying, the calmer the child feels and the less often she wakes.

To be able to stand this night life, you will ideally have to arrange to have a long nap during the day. Can you sleep at the same time the children nap if you're lucky enough that they both nap at the same time? What about a babysitter for one or the other of the children in order to break into their bad behavior when they are together?

People often hesitate to go to a child at night for fear they are setting up bad habits. But in most cases a new age produces new demands—or in your case we hope fewer demands—and you may find that a few months will improve your situation tremendously. We hope so.

FIFTEEN-MONTH-OLD REFUSES TO BE BATHED

Dear Doctors:

I have reached a point where I know I am doing something seriously wrong. In addition to my concern for my son, my own feelings of guilt are overwhelming to the point where I feel I have no right to start on another baby, which my husband and I have been planning on.

Freddy is Fifteen months old, healthy and normal in every respect. Until recently I prided myself on his wonderful, easygoing disposition.

Suddenly about two months ago he started to object to his bath. I ignored it the first time, thinking he would have forgotten by the next day. Not so! In fact, he screamed so that I had to use force in order to get the soap out of his hair. From that day on he has refused to have anything to do with water or washcloth except under duress.

I have tried going a week and more without bathing him, but that seems terrible to me, particularly since he has a sensitive skin, subject to allergic reactions. When he eats, all the food is rubbed into his hair, ears, etc. The very least I must do is get it out with a washcloth. But he sounds as though I am murdering him. And to tell the truth, I get so exasperated that I almost think I could.

I've tried sitting him on the kitchen drainboard and sponging him. I've tried diverting him. But he screams, I wallop. I am so ashamed I could die gladly. I've had nothing but contempt for women who shout at babies, let alone hit them. Now here am I, doing the same thing, and I don't know what to do. We are going to move soon. Do you think that will make things better or worse?

Your problem about bathing your son is not unusual. Many mothers report this same kind of difficulty around this age. Most children will accept some method of washing other than the usual one—such as sitting on the edge of a washbowl or drainboard. Apparently this doesn't work for you.

Our hope is that your move may indeed improve matters. It often does. However, if it doesn't, you may have to try letting someone else bathe your son. Whoever does it will have to approach things very cautiously, of course.

Don't make a head-on approach, but come at him with the washcloth from the back, starting at the back of his head. Also, keep him absorbed in some activity, such as playing with safety pins on a shelf at standing height, to take his mind off being washed.

Father often makes a wonderfully satisfactory substitute in a case like this. One mother reports:

> With all four of our children we solved the fear-of-the-bath problem in the same way. At the first sign of fear or balkiness, Daddy took over. He would fill the tub, get in himself, then invite the child to sit on his raised knees. What little one could resist? Above the water on such a safe perch there is nothing to fear, and before long there is much splashing and swishing up and down.
>
> Shampoos are easy this way, too. A child who is occupied with hollow plastic blocks and gaily pouring water from one to the other hardly realizes or cares that his head is wet or being rubbed.

We would not let this difficulty about bathing influence you against having another baby. It does not mean that you are not a good mother. It just means that you have struck a temporary snag. But these things almost always *do* work out eventually. Sometimes it is right after they seem to have reached their worst that the improvement comes.

FIFTEEN-MONTH-OLD THROWS EVERYTHING

Dear Doctors:

I must ask your help, as I am at this point quite frantic. My son, Fifteen months old, throws everything he can lay his hands on. This is so in his general play, but most particularly evident and unfortunate when he is in his high chair. And the habit seems to be getting progressively worse. He throws his cup, his spoon, and would throw his dish if it weren't held down with a suction cup.

If I take charge of the spoon and cup, he hits at them with his hands, of course spilling the contents. If I give him a toy to play with while I feed him, he plays with it for a short time and then throws it. And he dips into his dish with his hands and hurls the food as far as he can. Believe me, he, I, and the kitchen end up an unsightly mess.

I have tried taking him out of his high chair the minute he starts, giving him no more to eat. By the next meal he is ravenous, but that does not deter his throwing. Today when he spilled his entire glass of milk over both of us, I have to admit I slapped his hand, though I feel bad for having done it.

But what should I do? I have consulted what few books our library has on child care; I have searched my mind for a reasonable source of action. But nowhere do I find an answer. I need help.

This letter presents a good example of what we sometimes call a developmental or age-related problem—that is, a behavior which is typical of a certain age but which will in the normal course of development last for not more than a few months.

When the behavior is undesirable, as in your case, of course, you will do what you can to prevent it or work around it. Still, knowing that this troublesome behavior is not only temporary but normal and characteristic of the age in question can usually help you feel calmer about the whole thing.

Fifteen months is in many the high point for throwing behavior. The baby just naturally throws anything he can get his hands on. With toys, it often works best to tie them to his high chair. This may not please him very much, however. What he really likes is to throw things then have you get them and give them back to him.

The mealtime problem is more difficult but should not be unsolvable. To begin with, it might work out best if your son didn't have any dishes at all on his tray. You hold one dish or cup at a time, just out of his reach, as you feed him as rapidly as possible. There should be very little food in either dish or cup.

If possible, keep one hand free to hold down his hands (though this, of course, would work best if you yourself had three hands). If he throws or bats at the food too violently, the feeding situation should for the time being be terminated. Your son sounds like a healthy boy with a good appetite. We doubt that he will go entirely without food for long. Dry food which he can finger-feed himself might work out. He might take a bite or two before he throws it.

MOTHER DISTURBED BECAUSE YOUNG SON BITES AND SLAPS

Dear Doctors:

My son, Eric, difficult as a young baby, turned into a lovely person as the months progressed—very affectionate and good-natured, with quite a sense of humor. He laughs a lot and is generally bright and happy. The only thing that bothers me is that he often comes up behind me and bites me on the leg. He thinks this is very funny and goes into fits of laughter when I jump. Also, after he has given one of us a kiss, he is just as liable a moment later to swat us on the face. He does this, too, in seemingly high good humor, though a couple of times he has hit me in a temper. When he does that, I smack him sharply on the hands.

I smack him to try to teach him it is wrong. While it seems to stop him at the time, he will go right back to doing it again later on. Is there any way I can teach him not to do this? I'm afraid when he goes out to play with other children, he may hit or bite them.

The biting problem often begins in infancy, especially with early teethers, but as a rule it lasts only a few months. It is hard to know why one child continues with this and another resolves the problem by himself.

Try taking stock of all the situations when this occurs to see if and how the behavior could have been prevented. Does this biting occur at any special time? Or in any special situation? It may seem at random, but if you observe carefully, you may find that it occurs most at certain times of day—when he needs a nap, for instance, or when too many people are present or when he is overstimulated.

You have to realize that a parent often needs to give in more during this Fifteen- to Twenty-one-month period than later on. You may be making too many demands on him, not allowing enough for the inevitable rigidities and difficulties of this admittedly difficult age period. Children of this age often seem more mature and capable than they really are. We often unwittingly make too great demands of them.

There is no simple formula for preventing biting. A consistent policy of time-out in his own room after he has bitten somebody might possibly impress even one so young that it is not a good thing to do. The same will be true later on when he is playing with other children. Removing him from the group and isolating him whenever he bites will in all likelihood suggest to him that biting is not an acceptable behavior.

SHOULD YOU REMOVE BREAKABLE OBJECTS OR SPANK CHILD FOR TOUCHING THEM?

Dear Doctors:

I have an only son, Alec, a boy of Fifteen months. He's been walking for three months now and is constantly touching things he shouldn't. I realize all children do this, but my problem is this.

My family and friends insist I should spank him every time he touches something he shouldn't. I don't want to be rude and say he's my child and I'm not spoiling him. To keep the peace, I spank him, but with a heavy heart. It's against my better judgment and doesn't work as well as when I simply use a harsh tone.

Please tell me if I'm wrong in not spanking. I don't believe in a heavy hand for one so young.

No, you are not wrong in not spanking and in appreciating your son's immaturity and quite natural lack of restraint. However, your problem is a fairly common one. It occurs when a rather modern mother, who is kind at heart and also following current child behavior methods, conflicts with a more old-fashioned, stern family or group of friends.

It is, of course, possible to train a child as you would an animal and to "teach" him that if he touches things he shouldn't, he will get spanked. However, this is hard on the child and really unnecessary. We believe, as you do, that it is not only kind but fair to recognize the immaturity of a Fifteen-month-old. A child of this age or even somewhat older is not old enough to realize fully what he can touch and what he cannot. Therefore, it is wiser and more sensible to keep as many things as possible out of his way and also to keep him out of the way of as many things as possible.

A few things—ashtrays; books, perhaps; hot stoves, of course—we start in on. We speak sharply when he touches these and say "no, no." But it is better not to be saying "no, no" about too many things.

In your own house you can put a good many things away. You can also, by the use of small gates, keep him out of any specially vulnerable parts of the house. Could you manage for a while not to take him visiting so much? Or could you have him napping, or have a baby-sitter taking care of him elsewhere, when these people who are so strong on spanking are around?

We know it is embarrassing to disagree with friends and relatives, but you do have a right to bring your son up as you choose. And if you choose not to spank, you have lots of authority behind you.

EIGHTEEN MONTHS

EIGHTEEN-MONTH-OLD IS DEMANDING, EXACTING, AND
FRUSTRATES EASILY

Dear Doctors:

Our beautiful baby, who was such a joy to us for so
long, is now Eighteen months of age and a real drag. He
is constantly on the go. He is demanding. He is exacting.
He is too easily frustrated. What he wants, he wants now
and exactly as he wants it. He is all demand and no give.
He seems to have almost no ability to give in, to wait, to
adapt, or to modify his demands.

And so, in the interests of harmony, we give in. He
can't adapt, so we have to. He can't wait, so we wait
instead. He can't take "no" for an answer, so we reluctantly sometimes change our own "no" to "yes."

All the time, however, we have the nagging feeling
that we are spoiling him. If we give in and make things
easy for him, and put out of reach the things he isn't
supposed to touch, how is he ever going to learn to mind?

If we set up not only the physical arrangement of the
household but also his daily schedule so as not to frustrate him any more than is absolutely inescapable, how
is he ever going to learn to stand frustration?

Well, if you understand what an Eighteen-month-old is
typically like (and from your letter it appears that you do),
and if your giving in is part of a planned and intelligent
effort to respect and adapt to his immaturity, you are not
spoiling your son.

If you are giving in blindly to his every whim, you are
perhaps making a mistake. But if you know what you are
doing and why you are doing it, chances are that you, and
he, are safe.

Thus if you have said "no, no" as he touches some forbidden object, and you allow just that one last touch (assum-

ing it is not something really dangerous, like a hot stove) you are not spoiling him. You are recognizing the Eighteen-month-old's real need to go at least just a little out of bounds.

If, on a train or plane, you allow him to wander out into the aisle knowing (if this is the case with your particular child) that he will not wander more than one seat away—that isn't spoiling.

In fact, you may find out that if you give him an inch, he may not need to cry for a mile. His own ever-present reversal mechanism will often cause him to turn of his own accord and run back to you. Watch his new motor ability to make a rapid 180-degree turn to the opposite direction or to back up.

Above all, if you provide a lot of gross motor outlets for him, you may find that disciplinary problems of all kinds diminish. A good (safe) flight of stairs, preferably a carpeted one, which he can climb up and down, is the kind of thing you will find an absolute godsend in keeping him busy for long periods. It is also wise to provide a soft harness looped up in the rear, to be grabbed hold of as needed, especially when he is in a store or other public place.

With time and maturity, other methods of handling may be used. In a few months a little firm discipline will go a lot further and will be more effective than it is right now.

For the time being, however, you may have to accept the fact that "now" is your son's chief time word, and "no" is his main response to most things you ask him to do. You are not the only mother who has, reluctantly, discovered that her delightful baby does turn into somewhat of a "drag" when he hits the extremely demanding age of Eighteen months.

KEEP IMMATURITY OF EIGHTEEN-MONTHER IN MIND WHEN
DISCIPLINING

Dear Doctors:

I try to refrain from reading your column but sometimes I can't help glancing at it and then I'm angry for the rest of the day. Telling mothers that an Eighteen-month-old child cannot be disciplined is absolutely criminal, and the poor misled stupid creatures that some senseless mothers are believe you, and the results are disastrous.

Your daily articles sicken me. All this talk about child behavior is a lot of bunk. You always make excuses for bad behavior and tantrums, saying they are normal. You should put the blame where it belongs, on the lazy mothers who are so busy with their social lives that they don't take time to discipline.

All children are born without any bad habits, and if they develop them it is because they were allowed to drift that way. Start putting the blame where it belongs —on the mothers.

Shall we go over this bit about disciplining Eighteen-monthers just once more? Certainly an Eighteen-month-old can be disciplined. Our position is merely that you will get further faster if you keep in mind his inevitable immaturity.

The ordinary Eighteen-monther does not find it easy to "Come here, dear," unless he happens to have been planning to come here. Most are influenced more by actions (just picking them up and putting them where you want them to be) or by lures (holding out some attractive object that they want) than by merely standing at the other side of a room and calling them.

This doesn't mean that an Eighteen-month-old should rule the roost. It does mean that, when a child is so young that words do not entirely influence him, it's kind and reasonable to use other methods.

It does not mean that you let him get away with everything. It does mean that if you respect his immaturity you'll make out better. Certainly a totally "spoiled" child may indeed be the result of inadequate methods of child raising. But most people nowadays do appreciate that there are certain ages at which extremely negative, nasty, tantrummy behavior does come quite naturally to any child. And that it takes great skill, understanding, and patience to help him toward more positive and more acceptable behavior.

EIGHTEEN-MONTHER SHOULDN'T BE EXPOSED TO FRAGILE OBJECTS

Dear Doctors:

I am the mother of two sons, aged Eighteen months and Four months. I am eager to know if I made a mistake with my first one so I will not repeat it. George has always been very active. He started walking at Ten months and has had endless energy ever since. When he started walking, I removed everything from the coffee table and small ornaments from low tables instead of saying "no," and smacking his hands. There were enough things that couldn't be moved that were taboo. This was fine at home, but it was and is to a certain extent just too bad when I take him to someone else's house. He just goes wild, pulling things down. Of course, this is very embarrassing.

Many of my friends left everything in place with their toddlers, and they were so much better when away from home. Tell me, did I make a mistake in moving these things? Are some children worse than others about such things? Or will he be better off in the long run, even if he is not the so-called "model child" now?

In our opinion you have not made a mistake with George. Though it is possible with many children (particularly the extremely docile ones) to "train" them not to touch things, it is often a great deal of work, hard on both child and mother, and only partially successful at best.

The average child of Eighteen months or so can sometimes learn not to touch one or two extremely important things that have to be there anyway. But it is very difficult for him to discriminate among all the things in the ordinary living room between what can be touched and what can't. And even if he could and would discriminate, there are bound to be accidents. As, for instance, when he pulls himself up by a hanging table cover and thus pulls everything off the table.

We definitely recommend making it as easy as possible for any child under Two by keeping the more fragile things out of the way; or by keeping the children themselves out of rooms that contain too many things which can't be touched.

Of course, this does make it difficult to take them visiting with people who don't believe in putting things away. The ordinary child of Eighteen months is not restrained enough to be allowed to run around unsupervised in a household where things have not been put out of reach. The best solution is not to take him visiting. Or if you do, you or someone will have to play with him and give him the needed supervision.

You are quite right in thinking that some children are much less vigorous than others, don't get into things as much, and are much more easily cowed. Some children are very shy away from home and wouldn't dare touch other people's things. The basic personality may have more to do with their seemingly good behavior than does being so well trained.

Gradually as the child's own ability to inhibit and to understand what "no" means begins around Twenty-one months to Two years, you can increase your expectations. But we feel that in general it is kinder to the child to expect only what is reasonable.

MOTHER USES AFFIRMATIVE APPROACH WHEN DEALING WITH
TODDLER SON

Dear Doctors:

In regard to your recent article "Put Things Away From a Toddler," I would like to say that I wholeheartedly agree and would like to go one step further. We have a Twenty-month-old son, Joe. We have always used the positive approach with him rather than the negative. We have never had to say "no" to him—nor have we ever spanked him or slapped his hand.

For example, when Joe used to open one of my bureau drawers, I would say, "Close the drawer, Joe" instead of saying, "Don't open the drawer." Or when he liked to play with the doors in our apartment I would say, "Joe, close the door," instead of "Don't open the door." Likewise when Joe would touch or knock down an object on one of our tables or on the shelves, I would always say (and still do) "Please put (whatever it was) back on the table." That is, I never say "Don't touch that plate; no, Joe, that's breakable," or "Don't play with the ashtray."

In other words, Joe has always felt that he was playing a little game and/or doing the right thing and has, therefore, never broken any valuables. Concomitantly, we took our "good antiques" and put them out of his sight and reach from Ten months until Seventeen months. When we put them back in their usual places, he knew right away that they were not to be touched.

Once in a while I distract him with something else of interest. Besides the positive or affirmative approach, instead of the "no" or "don't" or slapping approach, I do keep a gate across the entrance to the living room. All of my friends think this is horrid.

We do this so that Joe can have free rein to all the other rooms and so that I do not have to watch him constantly. Of course, one must be consistent and rewarding, too, and therefore we always say "Good for Joe" when he does good things.

Thanks for writing. You have obviously done a wonderful job. This does credit to both you and your son, Joe. We often run into nursery school teachers who have the ability and patience, plus the ingenuity, to use methods similar to yours. It is perhaps less often that mothers (busy as they are with so many things) are inclined to show this kind of patience.

Your son seems to be especially tractable. We suspect that your methods would not work with every child. And we doubt that many mothers would be able, even if they wished, to entirely avoid the use of the word "no". In fact there are times when a good strong "no" is essential, especially in an emergency. Actually the gate on your living room door is one big "NO," but an acceptable one. And there are many children who respond better to the negative than to the positive. Remember that the infant can say "no" (Twelve-to-Eighteen months) long before he or she can say "yes," which often doesn't come in till as late as Three years of age.

OVERACTIVE EIGHTEEN-MONTH-OLD GIRL IS DRAGGING MOTHER DOWN

Dear Doctors:

Help! Help! I am a Twenty-seven-year-old mother. Before marriage I taught school and loved every minute of it. I was full of pep and energy and loved children. Always dreamed of having at least five.

Well, now I am married and the mother of an overactive, precocious Eighteen-month-old named Jennifer. I don't even feel like the same person. I just drag around the house, and by nightfall I am exhausted and discouraged. Five children? I was out of my mind.

Well, bless your heart. You do have a hard time, as you describe in your long letter (abbreviated here). But don't forget you're not the only one. Many children, from the time they are about Eighteen months till they are Four years of age, are not really horrible but are terribly demanding and time-consuming.

Children like Jennifer want your full time and attention. Some will even discriminate between the kinds of reading matter. They will allow their mothers to read light magazines, but not interesting novels or textbooks. They can seem to judge how much attention is being turned away from them.

In a way your husband is right when he says that Jennifer is your job. But a man who has not been trapped, hour after hour and day after day, cannot imagine what it is like not to be able to draw a free breath.

You can't really change a child like this but you can (usually) insist that you must have at least one or two afternoons a week off. It would be fair for your husband to take over one weekend afternoon. (Though the fact that we say so may not bring it about.)

At least get a baby-sitter, if you can possibly afford it. And eventually we hope you can arrange for nursery school. A child like this is a very real drain on a mother, but like pregnancy, it is something you have to live through. Chances are that any future child you may have might not be demanding in quite this same way.

MANY EIGHTEEN-MONTH-OLD CHILDREN REFUSE MILK FROM A GLASS OR BOTTLE

Dear Doctors:

We have a darling little boy, Eighteen months old, who at the present time has one fault that causes us much concern. He has never been willing to drink from a glass.

Suddenly, about two months ago, he refused his bottle. I offered it at every meal for a few days but he wouldn't touch it to his lips. I also offered him a glass, but he would just shake his head and push it away. I finally put the bottle away and just continued with the glass, which I am trying every mealtime, and occasionally with water or juices between meals. However, he has never accepted anything from the glass. I am wondering what to do. We've tried flavoring the milk; also tried not offering it at all for a few days.

Our youngster has another peculiarity about which most mothers of young children would say, "How wonderful!" He puts nothing into his mouth except occasionally his own fingers. If any food that I'm feeding him should drop onto his tray, he either rubs it away, or if it's in pieces, picks it up and throws it on the floor. He won't even put a cookie into his mouth. I am wondering if you think the above behavior might be the reason he makes no attempt to feed himself. Is there any way I can instill a desire in him to help with his feeding?

He gags easily on coarse food or foods with different textures. Is there anything I can do to help him overcome gagging?

It is not entirely unusual for a child to give up drinking milk from a glass or bottle around Eighteen months. They do take it up again later, but this recovery cannot usually be speeded up much by anything you do. However, sometimes children will accept things away from home, so you might try having someone offer him a glass of liquid when he is visiting. Also, he might possibly be interested in pouring liquid from a small pitcher into a cup or glass. We suggest having about a quarter of a glass of liquid in the pitcher, and after he has poured it, tell him that when he drinks it, you will give him some more to pour.

Your son seems to be the kind of child who cannot be hurried in feeding himself, since he does not have the usual strong hand-to-mouth reaction. He reminds us of another child we knew who would not feed himself even by Three-and-a-half and who was still on baby foods and gagged on solids. His mother finally had him feed his baby sister in order to establish hand-to-mouth behavior; and gradually he placed the spoon in his own mouth more and more frequently, until he was feeding himself entirely.

Another child did not accept solid food until he was Five-and-a-half years old, after being exposed to many birthday parties where only solid food was served. His mother had appreciated that it was characteristic of this child to be very slow in coming into any behavior, but that once he was ready he functioned well.

Undoubtedly you can give your son plenty of milk and other liquids in his diet (in puddings, soups, and so forth) so that he will receive an adequate amount even though he will not at this time take liquids from either glass or bottle. Perhaps he would accept very soft foods or extremely crisp foods, such as bacon, crackers or Melba toast, even though he may shun anything in between. We feel certain that your son will be feeding himself before too long. With children like this you tend to get further if you go along with them and respect their inhibitions.

SEVENTEEN-MONTH-OLD GIRL REJECTS MEAT AND VEGETABLES

Dear Doctors:

My granddaughter, Seventeen months old, will be visiting me shortly while her mother goes to the hospital to have another baby.

Libby has a bad eating habit that bothers me. She will not touch her noon meal of meat and vegetables. This has been going on for several months, and I am wondering if this will affect her health. Her mother prepares a vegetable and meat dish for her every day and offers it to her, but she just will not even taste it.

She has a good breakfast of cereal, banana, and milk. She has orange juice and vitamins. She will eat a fruit dish at night and milk—also toast and crackers and peanut butter. Is there any way I can teach her to eat vegetables and meat while I have her with me?

Admittedly your granddaughter will eventually need to branch out, but improvement is not going to come by offering her every day something she doesn't like and won't eat.

Instead of giving Libby a meat and vegetable dinner every noon, which she then refuses, we would very gradually introduce simple vegetables as carrot sticks and other things she can eat with her fingers. As for meat, crisp bacon is often the first thing accepted by children who are not meat eaters.

Of course, there are many who feel that meat is not a necessary part of everyone's diet. For the time being, try to think of good meat substitutes.

So, for Libby, we would have her noon meal like her other meals with just a little introduction of possible new foods. We doubt that in a week or two you can make any marked change in your granddaughter's feeding habits, but you might make a very small start.

EIGHTEEN-MONTH-OLD GIRL CLINGS TO MOTHER; NEEDS PROTECTION

Dear Doctors:

My Eighteen-month-old daughter, Laura, is anxious and timid when we visit other people's houses. She whines, "Mama, mama" and wants to be held constantly. When I leave her at home, even with a sitter she knows, she usually gets panicky and screams. She acts this way even if I go upstairs for a minute.

She has always been this way, ever since she was a colicky infant. When happy and secure she is active and gay, but she loses control quickly.

Would it be simpler if I just didn't try to take her visiting? Does she behave this way because I am oversolicitous and unsure of myself as a mother? Also, should I take away her bedtime bottle or wait for her to discard it herself?

This may not sound like a tremendous problem, but any mother whose child clings at home and cries and whines in public knows how wearying it can be.

Trying as it is, we know this kind of dependence represents a real need. So far as you can, try to avoid these visits, which your daughter finds so hard. We prefer to protect very young, timid children until they toughen up a bit.

If you picked out just one place which she found least difficult to visit, and returned to it repeatedly, she might begin to accept it. In the meantime, when you go out without her, do you insist on a formal good-bye? Although some mothers think it's more honest to say good-bye, in your case we recommend slipping out without making a fuss.

At home, when you have to be in a different part of the house, try to keep in contact by calling to her. For some, a walkie-talkie arrangement that keeps mother and child in touch seems comforting.

We doubt that Laura behaves as she does because of anything you have done. Your freedom will come gradually. But sometimes you can attain it faster by going a little more slowly along the way.

As for the bedtime bottle—we don't usually make an issue of this until a child is at least Two. By then even a small thing like a change in nipple may help the child to give up the bottle by herself.

But Laura is a clinger, and she may cling to her bottle as she clings to you. As the years go by, you'll probably face other aspects of this clinging and dependency. You'll have to meet each new problem as it comes, recognizing it not as a single, isolated issue but as part of a larger whole. Laura's clinging is her way of responding and part of her individuality. Only when satisfied at one stage will she move on to the next.

RICKY KEEPS MOTHER AWAKE MUCH OF THE NIGHT

Dear Doctors:

I need help, and badly! My son, Ricky, is One-and-a-half years old and a terror. As an infant he was colicky. And ever since his first birthday he wakes up at all hours and cries for hours.

Sometimes a bottle will quiet him but often not. I can't let him cry it out because of my upstairs neighbor. Also my husband doesn't like crying at night.

After going crazy all night, this little devil gets up and is crabby all day from lack of sleep. He does nap in the afternoon, and goes to bed about seven. I've tried keeping him up late, but it doesn't help.

Ricky has never slept a night in his life without waking four or five times to cry. For a while our doctor gave him medicine to try to help him sleep better but it didn't work.

I say that Ricky is crabby in the daytime. It's only fair to mention that I am too. I am getting to be a real crank from just sheer exhaustion. Please, please help!

Wakefulness at night is unfortunately more common, even as late as Eighteen months, than most people think. Some children can handle night wakefulness by themselves. Clearly your Ricky can't. You say that the bottle quiets him sometimes. Have you tried water play? Some will play with water in the bathroom basin and this seems to have a soothing effect.

Food, other than the bottle, often helps. It would be our hope that soon Ricky may be able to feed himself at night. Dried fruits may be your best bet. And for that matter, try to find an up-to-date pediatrician who may be able to discover some relationship between your son's diet and his wakefulness. Sometimes a good doctor-detective can trace such a relationship.

Until such a time, try, if you can, to see if more activity and exercise in the daytime may fatigue your son to the point at which he may be more tired at night. Do you take him on a good long walk (or carriage ride) at least once a day? Twice a day might be even better. Could you arrange for a baby-sitter to take over each afternoon so that you, hopefully, might get at least a catnap? This could help you sustain your dreadfully wakeful nights.

There are, of course, two points of view about night crying. Some feel that if a child finds out that nobody is going to respond, he or she will soon give up night demands. This is undoubtedly true of some easygoing and pliable children. With others—and we fear that Ricky may be one of these—the sooner you respond, the shorter the crying spell will be.

At any rate, your best bet might be to try if you can to find out if anything about Ricky's diet is causing him the kind of night discomfort which leads to waking and crying. Your second best bet may be to tire him out physically during the daytime so that hopefully he will need more sleep. Third, if you must get up so much during the night, you should try in every way possible to get a little sleep for yourself during the daytime.

And last of all, hold the hope that for your son, as for most, added age will bring more peaceful nights.

EIGHTEEN MONTHER ROCKS HIS BED

Dear Doctor Ames:

My problem is my Eighteen-month-old son, Larry. He is seemingly a happy, well-adjusted child who receives plenty of love and attention from us and from his brothers and sisters.

The problem is his persistent crib-rocking. He moves his bed across the room even though I have put rubber under the legs. It's getting to the point where it wakes us up at night.

We have tried telling him "no," and giving him a little spank, but he just waits till we are safely out of the room and starts again. This is very annoying and we don't know how to stop him. We fear it will interfere with his sister's sleep—she sleeps in the same room with him.

Larry sucks his thumb and drags a blanket around. This to me would seem to supply enough security without the crib-rocking. How can we stop it?

It's a long time since anybody asked us about rocking. Apparently the word has gotten around—there really isn't too much you *can* do to stop it.

Rocking is a perfectly normal stage of behavior in infancy. With many children it stops long before the second birthday. But when it persists, it's apt to increase in vigor until Two-and-a-half or even Three-and-a-half years of age.

About all you can do is to try to reduce the amount of noise it makes and the pleasure the child takes in it. You do this by being sure the crib is screwed tightly together and by putting something under the legs (as you have done) and setting the whole thing on a good thick carpet. This cuts down the action.

Sometimes a more prolonged going-to-bed hour leaves a child more tired and less tense. Sometimes more outdoor activity during the day reduces the need for rocking.

You say that sucking his thumb and dragging a blanket around with him *should* supply enough security for Larry without his rocking. I suppose the question is, How much is enough? Some children need much more tensional outlet than do others. It is Larry, not you, who decides how much he needs.

So far, his rocking apparently has not interfered with his sister's sleep, and it may not do so. Children get used to things quickly. And you see his sister is not handicapped by the feeling that the behavior is wrong.

One thing you might try is to set a metronome going at the speed at which his rocking usually occurs. This often satisfies a child's need for rhythm. Often these rockers are very musical, so see to it that your son has lots of musical experience—listening to records, being sung to, and so on. Provide a doorway swing and let him swing in it. Sing as you push him.

But since Larry is only Eighteen months old, our guess is that you may have to expect at least another year or two of this rocking before it will drop out of its own accord.

SENSITIVE BOY CANNOT SLEEP IN ANY BED BUT HIS OWN

Dear Doctors:

I have a son Eighteen months old. He will sleep only if he is at home and in his own bed. We couldn't get him to sleep in the car, playpen, or in someone's arms while on picnics or at drive-in movies.

Yesterday we were at a friend's house. He hadn't had a nap, so late in the afternoon he was so sleepy that I thought surely he would go right to sleep in their little girl's crib. He was so frightened when I put him there and left that he screamed and cried for half an hour and then went to sleep. He woke up half an hour later, though ordinarily he naps for two hours.

I got him up and he only wanted to cling to me. My husband and the other couple convinced me I should put him in the high chair and give him a cracker, for we were playing Scrabble. But he only wanted for me to hold him.

Finally they all said I was babying him and that I should let him sit and cry on the floor. They also said if he's so tired, put him back in bed. But I couldn't scare him all over again, when he still wasn't over his first scare. And my husband agreed with me on that.

I feel awful about it. But at the same time I think it's terrible that we can't go visiting and enjoy ourselves and have him nap wherever we are. I want to get him prepared for falling asleep in other places, but I don't know how.

And I don't know whether I should continue forcing him to sleep in other places, as scared as he gets. And should I leave him there to fall asleep finally from exhaustion when he is so afraid? My husband tells me I'm making a big baby out of his son and that he will come running to his mommy for every little thing when he is older too.

Your problem is difficult, but we think that you have a very good understanding of your son's personality. Your boy seems to be one of those extremely sensitive children who really cannot sleep in beds other than his own. Certainly one day he will mature to the place where he can be comfortable in other beds, but it will not be right away. It will probably be easier to get him to accept a baby-sitter in his own home (perhaps after you yourself have put him to bed), than to take him with you and try to adjust him to strange beds in other people's houses.

We do not consider this pampering. It is hard for some people to realize the depth of the fear which some of these rigid, immature children feel when they are expected to sleep in beds other than their own, or to use bathrooms other than their own.

We do not think you are making a baby of your son. We think he is babyish in his demands at the present time. It is natural for your husband and friends to feel that you are babying your boy—but very often a mother knows best.

MOTHER MAKES MISTAKE TRYING TO TOILET TRAIN
EIGHTEEN-MONTHER

Dear Doctors:

My daughter Penny is Eighteen months old and I feel she should be ready to be trained. Now possibly I am rushing the child and that is why I am writing to you, in the hope that you will advise me.

Excepting when she is in bed, I've started keeping her in training pants. She knows the words used for voiding and also knows that it pertains to her potty-chair. Regardless of this, she constantly voids on the floor, and comes and tells me after she's all through. And always seems proud of it.

She gets upset when I explain to her that she's doing wrong, and take her to the potty-chair and set her on it. I make a point of not raising my voice to her. But when

Daddy's around, he gets angry with me, because he feels I'm trying to train her too soon and that she's too young to know.

Maybe he's right. I'm hoping you can let me know. However I do feel that my husband shouldn't make such a point of it in front of Penny. But he feels I give children credit for understanding more than they do.

Please don't misunderstand. I have a wonderful husband who loves children and is very good to Penny and me.

Daddy is right. You are rushing things with Penny. Her present stage is a perfectly normal one. She should be proud, and you should be proud of her that she not only knows that the puddle on the floor was made by her but also that she is capable of telling you about it. But she has two more stages to go. She still needs to know when she is urinating and finally needs to know when she is about to urinate.

This will take time, and in the meantime, why make your life miserable by allowing her to make puddles all over the house? She will give you clues when she is ready, for she sounds like a knowing child. Two years of age will be plenty soon enough. What's your hurry? Put her in diapers and rubber pants. She may tell you when she is wet. And you in turn should compliment her by saying "good girl" for telling.

PATRICK IS A DADDY'S BOY

Dear Doctors:

My problem is that my Eighteen-month-old, Patrick, is not the usual mommy's boy. Rather he is a complete Daddy's boy.

He has always been afraid of strangers, even to the verge of hysteria. When this happened, as an infant, my husband would take him into a room alone and talk quietly to him.

Now he is okay with me in the daytime, but the minute his father comes home, he will have none of me. He wants his father to care for him, to play with him, comfort him if he falls down. Really, he's fine with me all day. It's just that when Daddy's here, he wants no part of me.

I'm afraid that the fact that he seeks comfort and attention from his father, rather than me, may later turn him into a homosexual. If you think this is all normal, it will greatly relieve my anxiety.

We do think this is all quite normal. In fact you may find that Patrick is even more definite in his demands that only Daddy "do" for him when he becomes Two-and-a-half and Three-and-a-half.

You say you aren't so much jealous as hurt at your son's preference for his father. Whatever you call it, you clearly don't like it. Everybody likes to be first with somebody, and once the honeymoon is over, your best bet is a very young child.

Even now your son is not rejecting you. Except when your husband is at home, you still appear to be first with your son, and you say that your relationship is good.

You worry about the later emotional effect on Patrick of being too much of a Daddy's boy now. Other mothers worry about the emotional effect on their sons of being too much of a Mama's boy. A little Freud can make an awful lot of mothers awfully anxious.

Also, don't forget that hundreds of mothers who have children who cling to them and won't let them out of their sight would give anything if their children would turn to Daddy once he came home, particularly if their husbands were as cooperative and kind with the children as yours is.

We'd say on the whole that you are very lucky. Make the most of a potentially happy situation and don't worry too much about homosexuality. Our bet is that your son will grow up to be quite normal.

You say that your husband calls your Three-month-old

baby "Mommy's girl" to make up for Patrick's favoring him. Both you and your husband will do best to stop emphasizing whose child is whose. Just take things as they come without all this labeling, which only serves to exaggerate any preference your children may quite naturally express.

BE SELECTIVE ABOUT TELEVISION WATCHING

Dear Doctors:

Is there any evidence that watching TV is detrimental to the emotional development of any infant? My son is now Eighteen months old. When he was a babe-in-arms I fed him often while watching TV as a relaxation for myself. I rarely watched programs of violence at that time, but they were often noisy. In the past four months he has begun to pay attention to the programs, until now it has become a daily routine to put the set on for the children's shows in the mornings. In the afternoon we watch cowboy films. These, of course, are filled with gunshots and fighting.

It seems to me that lately my son has been watching the fights and scary parts with rapt attention. I have taught him to say "bang bang" and laugh at the gunfighting, but the violence worries me. Do you think he is in danger of becoming so used to violence as portrayed on TV that he will think such actions are normal? Before TV, children usually didn't go to the movies until they were old enough to understand that it was all make-believe.

I must add that my son is unusually gregarious and happy. I am sure he is being educated, by osmosis if you will, through watching other human beings and animals that he would not see in real life.

In the past month he has become so fond of TV that he wants to drink his bottle on the sofa while watching it, and objects strenuously if put into his crib. He also loves to watch it at night when sometimes to comfort him we take him into the living room with us and let him watch for fifteen minutes or so. At that time, of course, there is often sadness or anger or violence being portrayed.

Do you think his rapt attention is due merely to the novelty of seeing all these strange sights, or is it possible that he is frightened? He does hit back sometimes when angry or when punished. Is that normal for his age, or is it related to seeing so much anger and fighting on TV?

Your son is hitting the TV stage early—too early. At first, very young children enjoy just watching the motion on TV, but your boy's interest now seems more specific. Our tendency would be to reduce greatly his amount of television watching and to be highly selective about what he does watch.

Nobody really knows for sure how much effect these things have on very young children. You obviously have found something (television) that interests and quiets your son. But we think you are using the medium in an unfair way. That is, you personally have managed to get him hooked on it.

We would even turn the set off, especially in the evenings when he wakes up, and try to quiet your boy in a more personal way. Of course, if the television is in some room far from his, and kept rather low, it won't be tempting him so much. Otherwise he will hear it and this may indeed disturb his evening sleeping, since he is so aware of it. We find that many television problems with children are made worse because parents don't want to give up their own favorite programs.

Television can have many good uses, but for an Eighteen-month-old, a little goes a long way.

TWENTY-ONE MONTHS

Your Twenty-one-month-old will not necessarily be all that much more mature or that much easier to live with than your Eighteen-month-old. But there will be changes and certainly progress. Here's a handful of typical letters from parents of Twenty-one-month-olds, examples of the kinds of problems one may meet in daily living with boy or girl of this tender age.

TWENTY-ONE MONTHS CAN BE HARDEST AGE FOR CHILD

Dear Doctors:

My Twenty-one-month-old daughter, Becky, is a real handful. If you can't answer this letter, I think I'll feel better just for putting all this down on paper.

As a former schoolteacher I have had experience with children, but it doesn't help me with Becky. Fortunately I have domestic help two days a week, but for the other five days she keeps me a virtual slave. Till she was Sixteen months old, I could not even pick up a newspaper without her demanding my complete attention.

Also, this attention must be given *in the house.* She hates to go outside. If I take her out and try to get her to play with other children, she screams and cries and holds on to my skirt.

And to make matters worse, she has begun to balk at eating. Meals are a nightmare. Fortunately she does have her security blanket and she chews on this, and sometimes it seems to help her.

My doctor advises me not to give in to her so much, but what can I do?

Twenty-one months can be one of the hardest ages because at this time a child's wants are even more definite than at Eighteen months and he or she still lacks words to express them. So, for the time being, go easy on your demands, give in when you have to, try to *guess* what Becky wants and needs and leave her as often as possible with the maid or baby-sitter. This is not the age to fight things out. When she is Two, she should be much less demanding and much easier to reason with.

For the time being, if you take her out, let her stay in her stroller since that is what she prefers. Don't force sociability.

Since she has been a good eater, go very easy in this area, and make as little issue as possible about eating. Sometimes it is just the color or texture of the food which children resist at Twenty-one months; sometimes as at Eighteen months, it is that you have given them the wrong spoon, or bib, or dish. Everything has to be *just so* for the Twenty-one-month-old or she's quick to let you know it. There are no simple rules for getting along. You just have to play it by ear and be a very good guesser.

A month later this mother tells us:

My, what a difference already, as I understand Becky a little better and relax myself.

You are right, too, that Becky is indeed much better with the baby-sitter than with me, so I'm getting her in for an extra day a week. This girl is very firm with Becky and really seems to manage her better than I do.

The outdoor problem is better since I don't make her get out of her stroller. And mealtimes are altogether better now that I let her choose her bib, spoon, and bowl and also the kind of cereal she wants. You said I would need both patience and courage in dealing with my daughter, and I think I am developing both.

MOTHER BOTHERED BY TWENTY-ONE-MONTH-OLD'S
RESENTMENT OF TOILET TRAINING

Dear Doctors:

I am writing in the fondest hope that you will consider my problem and advise me as I am desperate at this point. The problem concerns toilet training my Twenty-one-month old daughter.

In the many and various articles I read on the subject, they all agreed that too early training results in a trained mother and not a trained child. Therefore, I didn't attempt it until two months ago. Prior to that, noticing that she was occasionally dry at her regular time for a diaper change, I would put her on the toilet once in a while in order to acquaint her with it. A few of those times she urinated—after which I made a great fuss to show her how pleased I was. Feeling that she was still too young to attempt complete training, I did this only occasionally and not at all during the summer. However, when she was Eighteen months, I felt that I should begin regular training, and that's when the problem began.

She will not urinate on the toilet, *even though I know she could.* Whether she sits there five minutes or forty-five minutes, she waits until she is changed and downstairs—then wets her pants. I tried being casual, I've tried scolding, I showed her about the toilet—everything—but to no avail.

She is a bright, intelligent child—quick to learn. She walked at Ten months, began talking soon afterward, and has been outstanding in her progress. That is why I am at a loss to understand her reluctance to training. If I thought she wasn't ready yet, I would let the training go for another few months, but I'm afraid if I should stop now, it might confuse her even more.

I want to do the right thing, but at this point I don't know what is right or what is wrong. I discussed it with my pediatrician, but he was very busy and brushed it off with general training hints that I am already aware of.

If I could just get her to go once, I'm sure she would be all right.

We can encourage you by telling you that your daughter sounds as if she is on the verge of being successfully trained. When a child will sit on the toilet but then will not function until she has been removed and her pants or diapers have been put back on, that is usually the stage which occurs just before she is ready to stay dry and clean.

Whether you go on with your efforts or just skip the whole thing for a few months doesn't matter too much, except that continued efforts now may set up resistance in her and will continue to irritate and disappoint you.

We would be inclined to wait for a few months and then start in again. Your daughter is still pretty young. In most cases where the mother has taken things easily, it is around Two years of age or a little later that one can expect success.

TWENTY-MONTH-OLD HAS SLEEPING DIFFICULTIES

Dear Doctors:

I wish you could help me with a problem I have with my Twenty-month-old daughter, Melinda. Ever since we came back from our summer vacation, she refuses to fall asleep by herself. I have to sit with her and hold her hand until she is fast asleep. She also wakes up at night two or three times, and each time I either have to sit with her for half an hour or so or have to take her into my bed, where she falls asleep.

She started this while we were in the country and she was sleeping with her grandmother. Because we all were together, there was no special reason to be afraid of anything. She has never been left alone in her life.

I have tried to put her to bed and then go out of the room when she seems settled, but as soon as I leave, she starts crying so hard that she vomits, and I hesitate to have this happen because she is a very poor eater.

Should I put my bed into her room until she loses her fear, or what else could be done to overcome it? I would like to add that she has always hated to be by herself and never plays unless someone is with her and shows her how.

Many children begin to have sleeping problems around Twenty-one months of age, but these difficulties are often precipitated or exaggerated by a visit away from home in the second year of life. Often the problem might not have come up if the child had stayed at home. But now that it has occurred, it needs to be faced. Sleeping with Grand-mother has set up a pattern which your daughter natu-rally wishes to continue. Since she is by nature a dependent type of child, she will cling to this all the more.

You will have to be patient, and this weaning back to independent sleeping may take quite a while. Gradually, as she gets older, it may be that a light left on, and some food handy, will quiet her without your being there per-sonally. But for the time being it is probable that only the presence of some person in her room (not in her bed) will put her back to sleep. Which person is the best one to put her to bed should be your present concern.

It is not easy to wean a child away from demanding sleeping habits. Letting Melinda sleep with you might make things worse rather than better. Nor would we be inclined to move your bed into her room. Your best bet is probably to sit with her until she goes to sleep.

Sometimes a father will succeed in putting a child to bed better than the mother. Or even some outsider to whom the child will respond—that is, a baby-sitter whom she knows and likes—may have better luck than you and might be able to shift Melinda's sleeping into better line. Time is on your side. Most of these sleeping problems do not last forever.

YOUNGSTER FRIGHTENED BY RAIN, FIGHTS AGAINST NAP AND BEDTIME

Dear Doctors:

Our daughter, Tracy, is Twenty-one months old. A week ago, while we were entertaining friends, we had a bad rain- and windstorm. When Tracy's bedtime came, I undressed her and put her to bed, told her good night, walked out, and closed the door. After she had been in bed a few minutes, she started crying and calling for me. I went back to her room, asked her what was wrong, and she said, "Wind." I told her it was nothing to be afraid of and left again.

She became hysterical, and this time I let her come into the living room with us. About half an hour later I put her back to bed but left her door open. She began crying again. This time I let her stay up with our guests till they left.

Since then she says, "no, no," and starts to cry if bed is even mentioned. She refuses to go to bed for her nap or at night without her father or me sitting in the room beside her. During the night she wakes and screams. During the day, if she hears the wind blowing, she comes running to us and cries.

A fear of wind and rain seems to be felt by many children, especially girls, around Two years of age. But usual or not, of course, right now your daughter's fear is making a lot of trouble for you. It was most unfortunate that you had guests on the same night as the storm, especially when your daughter was just Twenty-one months old, an age when bedtime is often beginning to be difficult. It is as though the combination of the storm and the guests demanded too much of her all at once.

However, you should not in any way blame yourselves. We cannot protect children from everything. Every now and then, especially with the more sensitive child, something of this kind is bound to happen.

Tracy's present difficulty will not, we expect, be resolved quickly or easily. It may continue for as much as three months, with an up-and-down course. She may seem to be improving, and then a very small disturbance may set her back.

For the present you will have to give her all the support and protection you can manage. Of course, bed cannot be avoided altogether. But you will have to be as sympathetic and supportive as possible at both bed- and naptime. You may find that she does better at bedtime with her father alone than with you. Try out different routines and different methods of approaching the bedtime situation.

Some children are helped over this fear by having someone read to them. Or at least show the pictures from and talk about any book on rain and wind. One such book is called *The Storm Book* by Charlotte Zolotow. You may be able to find others. Or you can talk about the wind or even draw pictures of your version of the wind.

It is important to realize that these fears, though they may be in this instance caused by a special situation, are probably largely within your daughter's basic personality. She seems to be a sensitive child who is easily upset and frightened by new or difficult or violent situations. Thus, even after her fear of storms has subsided, you may find that she is easily frightened by further difficult or unusual situations. So you may for some years have to be rather on your guard and careful about trying not to demand too much of her in the way of meeting new situations and making new adjustments.

TWENTY-TWO-MONTH-OLD BITES HER GRANDMOTHER

Dear Doctors:

Will you please tell me how to stop a little one from biting and spitting at you? I am taking care of my granddaughter, Sara, while her mother works. This little girl is Twenty-two months old and really is so cute until she starts biting me. She walks up behind me without a warning. I am surprised to find that instead of putting her arms around me for loving, it is for biting. The more I reprimand her, the more she does it.

She will also walk right up and spit at me. Slapping stops her until she has had her cry, but back she comes for more.

In desperation, I tried a very little pepper on her tongue. She cried and cried and said, "No pep, no pep." Believe it or not, she bit my daughter on the ankle. Her mother slapped her across the mouth, but that is cruel. I can't do that.

Do you know of a way to stop all this? She is teething, but I just must find a good solution to stop her from hurting us all. She never takes no for an answer. She is very smart—walked at Seven months, traveled all over the country with her parents while her father was in service, knows her nursery characters, is learning her prayers now. Can you help?

Your granddaughter's behavior is not too unusual for a child of her age, a time when children are very apt to bite, less commonly to spit. Later on they hit, and later still they may kick when feeling angry or aggressive.

This, of course, does not excuse the behavior. But it is nevertheless interesting to note that in many things, even in the ways a child behaves when he or she is being naughty, it is to some extent possible to note predictable age changes. Behavior in the human infant tends to develop in the head end of the body first. Then, as the child grows older, it proceeds downward along the trunk. Thus spitting and biting often precede hitting and kicking.

This biting is hard to handle because, as you have observed, it comes so quickly and often without warning. You have to try not to turn your back on the child and to watch her very carefully. Whenever she seems about to bite, cup your hand quickly under her chin and bring it up suddenly and hard. Thus, if she bites anything, it will be her own tongue. This may seem cruel, but a few days of this, performed consistently, often helps a lot. It is rather time-consuming while you are doing it, but you may find it well worthwhile.

It is important to check and see if this kind of behavior occurs at any special time of day, say, when Sara is tired or hungry. If it occurs only at such times, you can be encouraged because then you have something to work on. You can, when she is tired, try to provide specially soothing and undemanding activities. Also, you can keep a watch out for the biting at this special time. If it occurs mostly with hunger, a little food given in time can in some children prevent the behavior. Increased age, however, will fortunately do more than anything else to help.

It is hoped that added age will stop the spitting as well as the biting. Spitting is hard to control. You might try the conventional time-out—banishing the child to some solitary spot away from people till the time (which you set) is over.

Whatever disciplinary measures you try in relation to either the biting or the spitting, try to remain as calm and emotionless as possible. Young children seem to feel rewarded even by negative attention, especially if it is dramatic. You must try to help Sara appreciate that these undesirable behaviors just don't pay off in any way.

In general we would try to fill Sara's time with positive and rewarding activities. This may reduce her seeming need to attract attention in these negative ways.

LITTLE BOY BITES LESS BUT PINCHES AND SHOVES MORE

Dear Doctors:

My Twenty-one-month-old son, Teddy, bites, pushes, and pinches other children whenever he gets the chance. At Twelve months, when he first bit others, I thought it was because he was cutting teeth. But now it is worse than ever. However, now he pinches and shoves more than bites.

My doctor says keep him at church only one hour instead of two. That is where he acts the worst. But even in the grocery stores or on the street he does these things.

I have tried spanking him, also biting him back, but it does no good. Should I have been more patient? I can't just stand and let him bite a child and then apologize, can I?

Do you think that his uncles' wrestling with him on the floor—which he loves—has made him rough?

Your doctor is right. It isn't unusual for a Twenty-one-month-old to act this way, and the best remedy is to cut down his opportunities for being with other children. However, we would not say one hour of church instead of two—we would say ten or twenty minutes or even no church. Teddy is too young.

And if you must take him on the street or to a store (admittedly sometimes necessary), keep him in a harness. Then, instead of just standing and letting him bite another child, you can yank him away.

You say you have slapped and spanked and bitten him back but it hasn't done much good. It seldom does. It isn't just that you should have been more patient—you should have, and still need to, keep him away from other children as much as you can.

You say he bites less now and pinches and shoves more. Pinching and shoving, you'll doubtless be glad to know, are more mature than biting and suggest that Teddy is growing up, even though slowly.

As to his wrestling with his uncles, it's hard to prevent some men and boys from playing too roughly with little children. So you may not be able to stop this. But at least try. Naturally Teddy can, and probably has to, play as roughly as possible with these big uncles of his. He is not yet old enough to realize that he can't treat little children in the same way.

From all you say, Teddy probably is going to be a good, tough, rough, masculine little boy, and there's nothing bad about that. It's just that at his present stage he is not ready to play with other children. He just doesn't have enough restraint. Added age will do more to cure his roughness with other children than spanking or biting him back or scolding.

YOUNGSTER'S HABIT OF THROWING AND HITTING UPSETS HIS MOTHER AND FATHER

Dear Doctors:

We have only one child, a boy, Twenty-one months old, who is amiable most of the time. We have been trying to teach him not to throw his bottle, food, or plate onto the floor when he finishes. We have met with very little success. We continually talk to him about it, and occasionally he will pick up the bottle and place it on the table. Mostly he picks it up and defiantly throws it farther. We have smacked his hand for this.

He also throws his toys around in the same manner. He may build ten blocks at a time, but if they should tumble, he gets the greatest pleasure out of throwing them all around. Also, we cannot break him of the habit of biting, no matter what we do or say. My husband thinks he is playing with me. However, he knows I dislike this because he really hurts, but he keeps on doing it.

Are we making too much of this? We have very little success in anything we reprimand him about. He deliberately does the thing again. He understands everything we tell him.

He is not an affectionate child at all. We both work, and he has a very good woman taking care of him. He likes her but doesn't show her any affection either. He has never kissed us and refuses when we ask. He will blow a kiss if we keep on begging for it. We both are affectionate to him and to each other at home. Can we handle him differently? Please help.

Our guess is that you have not had much experience with babies and little children. Since you work all day and are not with your son much of the time, you tend to take his behavior too seriously and to make too much of the things he does and doesn't do.

Let's take, first of all, his throwing things. It is quite right and normal, of course, for you to try to teach him not to throw things. But around Nineteen to Twenty-one months many children do throw just about everything that is not tied down. If you are not there to receive what they are about to drop, they let it go. Your son has not as yet built up a good give-and-take, which should come in another few months. Try playing the game of "Thank you" or *"Ta-ta"* with him, giving things back and forth.

As to his not being affectionate, this is possibly his basic temperament. Kiss or pat or cuddle him when you feel like it, but don't build it up or make any issue of his kissing you or accepting affection. Certainly don't keep on begging him for a kiss.

As to his hitting you, we would like to know what you do that seems to bring this on. Are you sure that you understand what he is asking of you? Twenty-one months may be one of the worst times for a mother to be away at work. So much happens during the day that the child later refers to in some way or other. A daylong shared experience with his mother could make communication easy. Some children cry when they are not understood. Others strike out. And often they persist in their demands until the other person understands. When language comes in more fluently around Two years of age, these kinds of problems will be much more easily solved. Your future with your son should be much easier than the present.

UNDERSTANDING AND PATIENCE IMPORTANT IN REARING A
MESOMORPHIC CHILD

Dear Doctors:

I wonder if anyone else felt the relief and reassurance (very badly needed) which I felt when I read your articles on the mesomorphic child. Every line and word you wrote described my child to a *T*. I was beginning to believe I knew nothing about child raising and that I was making a monster of my son. The only person besides my husband, my brother, and myself who can handle him is my godmother, and that is because she has the same type of child.

But did I say handle him? I'm always wondering if I am. There seems to be no end to the mischief he can get into. We don't dare leave anything around at night because if he wakes up first, he'll be into it. All medicines, naturally, have been put out of his reach long ago. I've had my lipstick smeared over everything. Lamps bro-

ken, too, which we have replaced with practically un-
breakable ones.

When he has to stay inside, I'm a nervous wreck, trying to stop him from jumping and running constantly,
though I am lucky that we have a summer cottage,
where he can run in and out and climb trees to his
heart's content. Also, I'm sure he'll be swimming before
long. He is absolutely unafraid of the water. When he
first saw the ocean, he ran right into it, shouting, "Water,
Mom, water."

Lately my problem is that he will not sleep in the
afternoon. That gives me a twelve-hour day of continu-
ous supervision. Even when he is outside, I'm always
peeping out to make sure he does not climb over our
second-story railing or fall downstairs. He'll always
manage to grab onto something by one hand, even when
he falls, hanging on until he regains his balance or
someone helps him back up.

His reflexes are extremely fast, but I'll tell you frankly
I've become very tired. In fact, I can hardly bathe him
at night or do my supper dishes. I wonder if you could
give me any advice on how to discipline and handle a
child like this.

In our opinion the matter of disciplining a mesomorphic
(highly energetic and strongly muscled) child most of all
involves an understanding of the child, and this you have
already. Since spanking or corporal punishment may have
only momentary effect and is at best a poor way of controlling or teaching a child, you must concentrate more on
providing a lot of legitimate outlets for his energy.

Sometimes you just have to pretend not to see what goes
on, for punishment for every offense would be a constant
court session. Praise for what good things he does may
help motivate him to repeat the good things. But his curi-
ous, expansive nature will always take him to things you
never dreamed of.

So keep your good nature if you can, and try to protect

your property—and your child—from physical harm. And see that you have as much relief as possible either through nursery school or a good baby-sitter. The greatest consolation is that matters get better as the child gets older and develops a little more responsibility about what he is doing. In the adult the mesomorphic drive often produces individuals of great enterprise and daring, who tirelessly and efficiently carry on their life's work.

In the meantime, here, as in so many problem situations, appreciate that there may be several reasons for difficult behavior and several kinds of solutions. It has been observed that certain kinds of foods tend to increase the activity and decrease the inhibitions of children like your son. A good pediatrician who is knowledgeable about nutrition might be able to help you here. As a start we would definitely reduce any intake of sweets.

WATCHING YOUNG CHILD GROW CAN BE A JOYFUL EXPERIENCE

Dear Doctors:

I know that many people write to you with their problems. I would like to write of my joy in my Twenty-one-month-old daughter, Sissela. I just can't imagine life without her. She grows more independent every day. Today she led our trip through the woods, walking ahead of her stroller and me. She knew exactly in which direction she wanted to go, toward the zoo, though this was her first walk on her own. Nothing could stop her determination of direction. She must already know the neighborhood through her carriage rides.

She walks well now, hardly ever falls, makes sharp turns, and takes backward steps as she dances with her father after dinner.

She keeps me company when I cook and plays with the kitchenware. Also, she is remarkably neat. When I drop a hanger, she picks it up for me and will not relax until I have replaced it. When I or she spills something, she makes it clear that it should be cleaned up. Sometimes

157

she does this herself. She picks up her father's socks from the floor and lays them on a chair. She even picks dead leaves from the clean white snow around our house and gives them to me. It is very funny because I have never taught her this.

She is very aware of what she is wearing and crazy about jewelry and all kinds of bottles. And the way she is flirting with her father is melting his heart.

The marvels of the world are opening up to her every day, and I see that she communicates with them more and more. She discovers how to use sticks with which she can touch leaves on the trees, or make holes in the snow. She won't touch the teapot because she knows it is warm. I can let her do and discover many things by herself because she is careful. When I definitely say, "no," as when she starts to climb the stairs, she stops. When she herself gets to the first step, she will say, "no, no," and come back down.

I have always tried not to intrude on her and let her just grow. I believe even more in this way as I see the results. The most mysterious thing to me is that nature's creatures are so reasonably well equipped. I may sound silly, but I trust nature.

And so do we!

chapter eleven

TRUE AND FALSE
QUIZ FOR PARENTS

1. A Seventeen- to Twenty-one-month-old is old enough to come when you call him. If he does not do so, he should be punished since discipline cannot start too soon. T F

2. By this age the child's attention span should be increasing. He should be expected to play with or attend to a single object for at least five minutes at a time. T F

3. Words are not the best way to influence a Fifteen- to Twenty-one-month-old. Physical handling may work better. T F

4. You should teach the child of this age not to touch forbidden objects. He or she is old enough now to learn to leave all breakable objects alone. T F

5. The Fifteen- to Twenty-one-month-old is more interested in pleasing himself than in pleasing you. T F

6. The child of this age is still better at gross motor than at fine motor activities. Fingers are not yet particularly skillful. T F

7. It is not unusual, in fact, is quite usual, for the Twelve- to Twenty-one-month-old to have a temper tantrum if frustrated. T F

8. Eighteen months is normally an age of unusually good physical equilibrium. T F

9. The Eighteen-month-old is fairly described as walk-

ing down a one-way street, often in the opposite direction from the one you have in mind.   T   F

10. The child of Twelve- to Twenty-four months is much interested in other children and loves to play with them. T   F

11. Using a harness on a Fifteen- to Twenty-one-month-old is a good way to control him when you are out for a walk.   T   F ⸝

12. Since the Eighteen-month-old is a furniture mover, it will work best not to have too much furniture which can be moved, in his room.   T   F

13. Most Eighteen- to Twenty-one-month-olds can stay dry all day, even though not at night.   T   F

14. A pull toy, at this age, may be one of the child's favorite playthings.   T   F

15. By Twenty-one months of age a child should no longer be sucking his or her thumb.   T   F

16. At Eighteen months the child's appetite should be larger than when he was an infant.   T   F

17. Few children are ready to stay dry till they at least notice the puddles they have made.   T   F

18. If the Eighteen- to Twenty-four-month-old likes to take all his clothes off and run around with nothing on, there is obviously something wrong with him.   T   F

19. If you spend a lot of time teaching and playing with your One-year-old, he will develop much faster than if you don't.   T   F

20. If you spend a lot of time playing with your pre-schooler, he will be happier and may function more effectively than if you don't.   T   F

21. Your child's emotional state and personality depend entirely on the way you treat him.   T   F

22. Fathers should be willing to play with their children whenever asked to do so, whether they feel like it or not. T   F

23. As the child moves into the Fifteen- to Eighteen-month age zone, he should be easier to live with than when he was an infant.   T   F

24. A Fifteen-month-old baby is too old to be carried. T F

25. A Fifteen-month-old may be safest if he or she is not let loose in the living room, but it is protected by little gates. T F

26. Taking the Fifteen- to Twenty-one-month-old for long carriage rides is an excellent way to entertain him. T F

27. Twenty-one months is not too early to begin making serious efforts at toilet training. T F

28. In a day care or nursery school situation, the Eighteen- to Twenty-one-month-old "talks" more to other children than to any adult present. T F

29. Eighteen months in many children is one of the more oppositional of the preschool ages. T F

30. As the child moves on from Twenty-one months to Two years of age, life usually becomes easier for all concerned. T F

CORRECT ANSWERS TO TRUE AND FALSE QUESTIONS

1F; 2F; 3T; 4F; 5T; 6T; 7T; 8F; 9T; 10F; 11T; 12T; 13F; 14T; 15F; 16F; 17T; 18F; 19R; 20T; 21F; 22F; 23F; 24F; 25T; 26T; 27F; 28F; 29T; 30T.

APPENDIXES

appendix A
Toys or Play Objects

Any group of small objects in a large container
Bells
Blocks, large wooden or small colored
Books
Chair swing for doorway
Chest of drawers (small)
Color cone—graduated wooden rings on a peg
Dishes, nonbreakable
Dolls
Hammer, light rubber, or any other pounding toys
Jack-in-the-box
Music box
Pail and shovel
Plastic blocks with cutouts into which can be fitted plastic animals, people, objects
Plastic blocks in geometric shapes (triangle, square, circle, etc.) with holes into which fit plastic rods
Play-Doh
Pocketbook
Pots and pans with covers
Pull toys, push toys
Rocking horse
Soft woolly animals
Stairs
Toy shoes
Watch, large, loudly ticking, with highly visible hands
Wrist bells

appendix B
Books for Fifteen- to Twenty-one-Month-olds

Aliki. *Hush Little Baby.* Englewood Cliffs, N.J.: Prentice-Hall, 1968.

Anglund, Joan Walsh. *The Adam Book; The Emily Book;* and *The Emily and Adam Book of Opposites.* New York: Random House, 1979.

Brown, Margaret Wise. *Goodnight Moon.* New York: Harper & Row, 1947.

Bruna, Dick. *The Apple.* New York: Methuen, 1975.

———. *The Fish.* New York: Methuen, 1975.

———. *The Little Bird.* New York: Methuen, 1975.

———. *Out and About: A Dick Bruna Zig Zag Book.* New York: Methuen, 1980.

Chorao, Kay. *Baby's Lap Book.* New York: Dutton, 1978.

Craig, Helen. *The Mouse House.* New York: Random House, 1979.

Dodson, Fitzhugh. *I Wish I Had a Computer That Makes Waffles.* La Jolla, Calif.: Oak Tree Press, 1978.

Ford, George. *Baby's First Picture Book.* New York: Random House, 1979. Cloth.

Fujikawa, Gyo. *Babies.* New York: Grosset & Dunlap, 1978.

Johnson, John E. *My First Book of Things.* New York: Random House, 1979. Cardboard.

———. *The Me Book.* New York: Random House, 1979. Cloth.

———. *The Sky Is Blue, The Grass Is Green.* New York: Random House, 1980. Cloth.

Kunhardt, Dorothy. *Pat the Bunny.* New York: Simon and Schuster, 1967.

McKie, Roy. *The Alphabet Block Book.* New York: Random House, 1979.

Miller, J. P. *The Cow Says Moo.* New York: Random House, 1979. Cloth.

———. *Sniffy the Mouse.* New York: Random House, 1980.

Mother Goose. New York: Grosset & Dunlap, 1978.

Parr, John. *Baby Animals.* New York: Random House, 1979. Cloth.

Pfloog, Jan. *Puppies.* New York: Random House, 1979.

Scarry, Richard. *Huckle's Book.* New York: Random House, 1979. Cloth.

Shortall, Leonard. *Zooanimals.* New York: Random House, 1980. Cloth.

Skaar, Grace. *What Do the Animals Say?* New York: Scholastic Book Service, 1973.

Smollin, Michael J. *Meet Strawberry Shortcake and Her Friends.* New York: Random House, 1980. Cloth.

Steiner, Charlotte. *My Slippers Are Red.* New York: Knopf, 1957.

Wells, Rosemary. *Max's First Word.* New York: Dial, 1979. Cardboard.

———. *Max's Toys.* New York: Dial, 1979. Cardboard.

———. *Max's New Suit.* New York: Dial, 1979 Cardboard.

Watanaby, Shigeo. *How Do I Put it On? Getting Dressed.* New York: Collins, 1979.

Wilkin, Eloise. *Nursery Rhymes.* New York: Random House, 1979.

Zolotow, Charlotte. *The Storm Book.* New York: Harper & Row, 1952.

appendix C
Books for Parents

1. Ames, Louise Bates. *Child Care and Development.* Philadelphia: Lippincott, 1979.
2.———. *Parents Ask.* Syndicated newspaper column distributed through the Gesell Institute, New Haven, Connecticut.
3. ———, and Chase, Joan Ames. *Don't Push Your Preschooler,* rev. ed. New York: Harper & Row, 1981.
4. ———; Gillespie, Clyde; Haines, Jacqueline; and Ilg, Frances L. *The Gesell Institute's Child from One to Six.* New York: Harper & Row, 1979.
5. ———, and Ilg, Frances L. *Your Two-year-old.* New York: Delacorte, 1976.
6. Benning, Lee. *How to Bring Up a Child Without Spending a Fortune.* New York: McKay, 1975.
7. Braga, Laurie, and Braga, Joseph. *Learning and Growing: A Guide to Child Development.* Englewood Cliffs, N.J.: Prentice-Hall, 1975.
8. Brazelton, T. Berry. *Infants and Mothers.* New York: Delacorte, 1969.
9. ———. *Toddlers and Parents.* New York: Delacorte, 1974.
10. Calladine, Andrew, and Calladine, Carole. *Raising Siblings.* New York: Delacorte, 1979.
11. Coffin, Patricia. *1, 2, 3, 4, 5, 6: How to Understand and Enjoy the Years That Count.* New York: Macmillan, 1972.
12. Comer, James P., and Pouissant, Alvin F. *Black Child Care: How to Bring Up a Healthy Black Child in America.* New York: Simon and Schuster, 1975.

13. Crook, William G. *Tracking Down Hidden Food Allergy.* Jackson, Tenn.: Professional Books, 1979.

14. Dodson, Fitzhugh. *How to Parent.* Los Angeles: Nash, 1970.

15. ———. *How to Discipline with Love.* New York: Rawson, 1977.

16.———. *How to Grandparent.* New York: Lippincott/Crowell, 1980.

17. Gersh, Marvin J. *How to Raise Children at Home in Your Spare Time.* New York: Stein and Day, 1966.

18. Gesell, Arnold; Ilg, Frances L.; and Ames, Louise Bates. *Infant and Child in the Culture of Today,* rev. ed. New York: Harper & Row, 1974.

19. Ilg, Frances L.; Ames, Louise B.; and Baker, Sidney M. *Child Behavior,* rev. ed. New York: Harper & Row, 1981.

20. ———. *Parents Ask.* New York: Harper & Row, 1962.

21. Jones, Hettie. *How to Eat Your ABC's: A Book About Vitamins.* New York: Four Winds Press, 1976.

22. Kohl, Herbert. *Growing with Your Children.* Boston: Little, Brown, 1979.

23. Lansky, Vicki. *The Taming of the C.A.N.D.Y. Monster.* Wayzata, Minn.: Meadowbrook Press, 1978.

24. LeShan, Eda. *How to Survive Parenthood.* New York: Random House, 1965.

25. Levine, Milton I., and Seligman, Jean H. *The Parents' Encyclopedia of Infancy, Childhood and Adolescence.* New York: Crowell, 1973.

26. Olness, Karen. *Raising Happy, Healthy Children.* Wayzata, Minn.: Meadowbrook Press, 1977.

27. Samuels, Mike, and Samuels, Nancy. *The Well Baby Book.* New York: Summit Books, 1979.

28. Smith, Lendon B. *The Children's Doctor.* Englewood Cliffs, N.J.: Prentice-Hall, 1970.

29. ———. *Improving Your Child's Behavior Chemistry.* Englewood Cliffs, N.J.: Prentice-Hall, 1971.

30. ———. *Feed Your Kids Right.* New York: McGraw-Hill, 1979.

31. Stevens, Laura J., and Stoner, Rosemary. *How to Improve Your Child's Behavior Through Diet.* New York: Doubleday, 1979.

INDEX